Cicerone
County Walking Series

WALKING IN SUSSEX

by

Kev Reynolds

*They only know a country who are acquainted with its
footpaths. By the roads, indeed, the outside may be seen;
but the footpaths go through the heart of the land.*
(Richard Jefferies)

CICERONE PRESS LTD.
MILNTHORPE, CUMBRIA
www.cicerone.co.uk

© Kev Reynolds 2000
ISBN 1 85284 292 X
A catalogue record for this book is available from the British Library

ACKNOWLEDGEMENTS

I am grateful to the stalwarts of various rambling clubs in Sussex for their vigilance in regard to access problems, and to the many unnamed local historians whose leaflets, usually on display or for sale in village churches, provide interesting background information about their local communities. As ever, my wife accompanied me on almost every walk and added to the pleasures of each mile. Our good friends Alan and Morna Whitlock also joined us on occasion, and it is to them I dedicate this further collection of what they term 'Kev Walks'. May this book lead them on many more happy days walking in Sussex.

Kev Reynolds

Cicerone guidebooks by the same author:

Walking in Kent Vols I & II
The South Downs Way & The Downs Link
The Wealdway & The Vanguard Way
The Cotswold Way
Walking in the Alps
Walks in the Engadine - Switzerland
The Valais
The Bernese Alps
Ticino - Switzerland
Central Switzerland

The Jura (with R. Brian Evans)
The Alpine Pass Route
Chamonix to Zermatt, The Walker's Haute Route
Tour of the Vanoise
Annapurna - a Trekker's Guide
Everest - a Trekker's Guide
Kangchenjunga - a Trekker's Guide
Langtang & Helambu - a Trekker's Guide
Walks & Climbs in the Pyrenees

Front Cover: The Seven Sisters, where the South Downs meet the sea

CONTENTS

THE WALKS

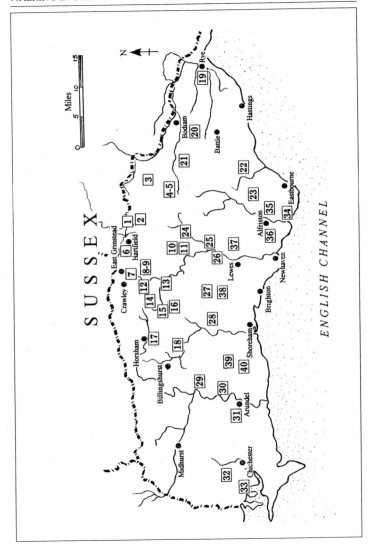

INTRODUCTION

"It is not only what you actually see along the path, but what you remember to have seen, that gives it its beauty."
(Richard Jefferies 1848-1887)

In a walk of less than five minutes from where I write these words, I can be seated beneath a holly tree whose branches act as a parasol in summer and an umbrella in winter, and from there gaze across a landscape of generous proportions that never fails to gladden the heart. Far below the Weald stretches from east to west, its rich green pattern of woodland and meadow darkened here and there by cloud-shadows, while an undulating line is drawn on the southern horizon that eases pastel blue against the sky. But at times, and in certain lights, that bounding rim of hills glows purple to emphasize its heathland nature. More than one hundred and seventy years ago William Cobbett called that heather-clad ridge "the most villainously ugly spot I saw in England."

I love it!

So do countless others who, like me, flock to Ashdown Forest throughout the year to walk through the heather and gorse, or to simply lounge among stands of pine, to breathe the fresh clean breeze that shakes the needles, to hear the chattering of anxious finches, and to absorb the magic of a 360 degree panorama that has the North Downs as one horizon, and the immensely seductive wall of the South Downs as the other. Nine-tenths of this panorama belongs to Sussex. Through it and across it routes have been woven for unnumbered generations as southern man's first roads: not roads as we know them, but paths and trackways whose purpose was to aid the hunter, home-maker, flint-miner, iron-worker, soldier, farmer, smuggler, timberman... It is only in comparatively recent times that man has taken to the byways for the sake of recreation pure and simple.

Only in comparatively recent times have we had *time* to go wandering for pleasure. Time and opportunity - and the *need*.

There's no better way of shaking off the stresses of modern living than by turning one's back on an urban environment and stepping away from tarmac, concrete and brick onto a trail that leads to whispers of the past. Sussex has footpaths aplenty that do just that. Footpaths that delve into a rural heartland, that follow streams and rivers, that trace the bank of hammer pond and lake, entice among copse, woodland and forest, seduce onto hilltop and along ridge-crests to offer a walk in the sky. Footpaths that have the sea all glistening to one side, sheep-grazed downland on the other. Footpaths that plunge into deep, mossy ghylls haunted by shadows, or meander through wide open spaces where wind-bent trees grow stunted before the gales of winter. And always, always, it seems, with scenes to charm every sense along the way.

" Always get over a stile, is the one rule that should ever be borne in mind by those who wish to see the land as it really is - that is to say, never omit to explore a footpath, for never was there a footpath yet which did not pass something of interest."

So wrote Richard Jefferies in the latter half of the 19th century. "To see the land as it really is" is just one of the rewards we gain when out walking. The motorist will, at best, catch but a fleeting glimpse of that land beyond the roadside verge, but of course he'll be divorced from its reality. The cyclist may cover a greater distance than the walker and capture for a brief moment in time the scent of hedgerow or meadow in passing - if he's lucky enough to be free of traffic fumes, that is. But where he can go will be only slightly less restricted than the motorist. The horse-rider may have a wider field of vision, but only the walker has direct contact with the land, can move at a pace sedate enough to absorb the very essence of the landscape, the opportunity to stop in an instant to spy on rabbit or vole going about its daily business unaware of his presence. For if the walker's senses be tuned, he can capture the rich diversity of sound, scent, touch and taste of the countryside through which he travels. In short, to see the land as it really is.

But since you picked up this book and have read this far, you'll know the joys of walking anyway! My purpose here is to share with you some of the joys my wife and I have experienced over the years whilst walking in Sussex - days of sheer delight - in the hope that you too will gather as much pleasure as we have.

Forty walks (plus 16 variations and suggestions for longer routes) are not many among the wealth of opportunities available, yet they provide a sample of what the county has to offer. There's plenty of variety - not only in landscape terms, but historically and culturally too - and each walk is a gem in its own right. None is of great length - the longest of the main walks is $9^{1}/_{2}$ miles, the shortest just $3^{1}/_{4}$ - but distance has no real bearing on the amount of pleasure to be harvested. If you have a real interest in the land, and the life of the countryside through which you journey, then a modest four-mile walk can lead to a full day of interest and enjoyment. Let those who see challenge in multi-miles devoured beneath their boots charge into the distance. Walks described within these pages are for those in a relaxed frame of mind. These days I prefer to wander rather than march, to dream beside a brook, taste a leaf or two, lean on a gate and *wear* the view!

*   *   *

Walks contained in this book describe paths and tracks as found on research, nearly all of which are accurately represented on the Ordnance Survey maps quoted. However, the Sussex countryside is no more static than that of any other county in Great Britain, and changes are inevitable over the period in which this guidebook is likely to be in print. Pressure is on the county to submit more of its green acres to housing; golf courses appear seemingly overnight; agricultural uses change; field boundaries disappear, or alter shape and, it must be said, a few (just a few) landowners actively try to deter walkers from their estates. Many more than just forty walks were tackled on research, but some were discounted because the paths were poorly defined or blocked completely, and although some of us will force passage when convinced of the line of a right of way, I want readers who follow my route descriptions to enjoy each step of their walk without fear of confrontation or the need to battle with obstructions.

However, should you discover that a section of any walk described here has been altered drastically, for one reason or another, I would appreciate a note giving specific details, and it will be checked in advance of any subsequent edition. Correspondence may be addressed to me c/o Cicerone Press, 2 Police Square, Milnthorpe, Cumbria LA7 7PY.

Kev Reynolds

Knowlands Wood

During April and May we have been happy to allow free access throughout the wood, and hope to go on with this in future years. We hope you have enjoyed the windflowers and bluebells, and the singing of the summer bird visitors - chiff chaffs and other warblers, cuckoos and even a nightingale

Thank you for the way you have all been so good about not leaving litter. We have hardly had to pick up a cigarette end. [There was one isolated instance of vandalism, by no means representative]. Thank you, too, for your appreciative comments.

For the rest of the year, June to March, we do ask you to keep to the public footpaths. We trust you understand. We have put up some new yellow arrows, to make it clear where the public footpaths are. There is one through the wood and lots through Knowlands Farm.

Nick and Harriet Lear   June 1998

Where walkers are welcome

SUSSEX - A WALKER'S COUNTY

"The Weald is good, the Downs are best"
(Rudyard Kipling 1865-1936)

Kipling's love of Sussex was such that he spent 34 years at Batemans, near Burwash, and the county's natural features were reflected in a number of his poems. He wrote of the South Downs, and their "bare slopes where chasing shadows skim," with such potent imagery that an accord is struck with anyone who has gazed or wandered upon them. In the same poem ('Sussex' - written in 1902, the year he moved to Batemans) he described "belt upon belt, the wooded, dim blue goodness of the Weald" - that reference serving as a reminder that Sussex is the most heavily wooded of all southern counties. But what may seem the "dim blue goodness" from a distant view is revealed as a luxurious canopy consisting of a dozen shades of green when wandering a footpath through those self-same woods. Add to those greens the pink or purple splash of rhododendron, a feathery frieze of rosebay willowherb at the tail-end of summer, or the grey/dusty-white carpets of early spring flowers, and that dim blue goodness is transformed from a poetic backwash to a vibrant and multi-textured reality - not to mention the complex and startling splendours of autumn's rich colouring.

When Kipling wrote that "the Weald is good, the Downs are best" he was perhaps voicing a popular prejudice. But while the Downs have their own impressive beauty, the Weald is in truth no second best. Different, certainly, but in no way is it inferior to the South Downs. Indeed, in aeons past the Weald was covered by the same dome of chalk, but millions of years' worth of rain and frost have worn away the central roof to expose a vast belt of wood and meadowland, now contained between the North and South Downs. Hilaire Belloc, the only real challenger to Kipling's poetic love of Sussex, advised "a man with leisure desiring to understand what is left of the ancient kingdom … [to] wander inland for a fortnight, taking no direction but exploring from village to village, avoiding towns and sampling the whole Weald from the Hampshire border to Kent."

The Downs and the Weald are, indeed, the main topographical features of Sussex, and by far the majority of our walks are located among them - although in the extreme east and west of the county the low coastal plain is also represented. And since topography defies the political boundaries that divide the county into East and West, so too will this guidebook and the walks described turn a blind eye to local government's division of responsibility. First, though, a brief outline of the county's main geographical features, for these provide the bare bones of our walks, the incentive and inspiration.

ASHDOWN FOREST & THE HIGH WEALD

The High Weald Area of Outstanding Natural Beauty cuts across much of the county and includes part of Surrey and Kent where they scuff against northern Sussex with a series of steep, wooded ridge-lines. The High Weald is a watershed full of dramatic beauty, its valleys drained by modest streams and rivers that become the major waterways of southern England - the Medway flowing to the Thames, the Ouse, Arun and Rother draining to the Channel - with sandstone outcrops lining some of these valleys, and charming lakes or ponds adding magnetic appeal to others, while remnants of primeval woodland survive in the forests of Balcombe, St Leonard's, Tilgate and Worth.

In Roman times the Weald was covered by the huge forest of Anderida which stretched for 120 miles across south-east England. This was seen as a natural gift, not only to ship-builders (it took 36 acres of woodland to build the *Mary Rose* in Tudor times), but also to the iron-makers who felled the great oaks to feed the furnaces of the industry which peaked in the first half of the 17th century. Thanks largely to that industry the Sussex Weald in particular became home to wealthy landowners who gave the area many of its grand houses and estates, some of which are now open to the public, others being viewed from footpaths that skirt them. Sunken pathways and drovers' tracks wind through landscapes of unique beauty just as they have for centuries, leading to vantage points from which no end of unspoilt panoramas are the norm.

Ashdown Forest crowns one part of the High Weald ridge system. It once covered 15,000 acres, but much of its woodland cover has gone now, and in its place acres of heather and gorse sweep across open hills and down into steep-sided ghylls where rust-coloured brooks carve out mini canyons, greened with moss and fern, which twist this way and that. Once a royal hunting reserve, today the Forest is freely grazed by sheep that stray onto the few roads that cross it. Deer emerge at dawn and dusk, and adders sun themselves on the open rides. It's a splendid region for the lover of distant views, and for those who enjoy wandering with no particular aim. But it has to be said that with so many footpaths, rides and trackways unmarked on any Ordnance Survey map, and with few waymarks or finger posts to give direction, it is not always easy to follow a specific route. One June morning I came across a family from Belgium who had been attracted to Ashdown Forest by a tourist authority brochure and, armed with an out-of-date OS map and a walks leaflet, had set out to explore. Three hours after leaving their car they'd become hopelessly lost among a labyrinth of trails not shown on their map. They could not even remember the name of the car park where they'd started, but with a bit of detective work and 'local knowledge', I managed eventually to reunite them with their vehicle. The moral here, if you plan to go exploring, is make first a note of where you leave the car, take a good map and compass - and enjoy the challenge!

While the greater part of south-east England consists of 'managed' landscapes, Ashdown Forest gives an impression of wildness, and may be likened to the remoter regions of Exmoor. But elsewhere in the High Weald pockets of farmland break the woodland cover, and there are large reservoirs too that add, rather than detract from the overall scene. Ardingly Reservoir, which stretches almost from Ardingly to Balcombe, has mellowed among the series of shallow valleys that were dammed to form it. Crested grebe breed there, and a shoreline footpath provides opportunities for bird-watching. This path has been adopted for one of the walks in this book, while Weir Wood Reservoir, visited on another of our walks, is not quite so easy of access, but when seen from a neighbourhood hilltop, it could be taken for a natural, rather than a man-made, lake.

Villages of white weatherboarded or tile-hung cottages populate the High Weald country, their slender-spired or sturdy-towered churches often giving the only hint of their presence when glimpsed from afar. Some of our walks begin in such villages, or make a point of straying to them - perhaps for mid-walk refreshment, or simply because they form an integral part of the Sussex scene. Hartfield, for example, with its lovely (though too busy) main street, a wonderful entrance to its churchyard, and scenes straight out of *Winnie the Pooh* on its doorstep. Then there's Horsted Keynes, better known to some for its station on the Bluebell Line, but apart from which it's an attractive and interesting place with a long village green, two pubs and a fine church, and a string of hammer ponds just outside. Or lovely West Hoathly, founded in Saxon times, Slaugham with its trim line of cottages and the remains of an Elizabethan mansion which once stood in 700 acres of deer park, or Mayfield, one of the very best in the county, with its distinguished High Street, one-time archbishop's palace, splendid Tudor inn, and a rich assortment of footpaths splaying from it. Each of these, and many others, hold the very essence of Sussex down the ages, form a link between the past and present, and give hope that the county's future will not be entirely lost to insensitive development.

THE LOW WEALD

Between the High Weald and the South Downs, and running west from the Pevensey Levels, lies the broad valley known as the Low Weald, sometimes called the Vale of Sussex. Notorious for its heavy, glutinous clay and its terrible roads, Daniel Defoe once described seeing "an ancient Lady, and a Lady of very good Quality, I assure you, drawn to church in her coach and six oxen; nor was this done in frolic or humour, but mere necessity, the way being so stiff and deep, that no horses could go in it."

The agricultural heritage of this part of the county is marked by the effort involved in working the land, its fields quickly becoming parched and cracked in the heat of summer, but waterlogged, frosted or fogbound in winter. The pasturelands of the Pevensey Levels have been sliced with drainage dykes, as have the water-meadows at the western end of this low-lying quarter - the patchwork country overlooked from the crest of the Downs as one gazes north towards the distant rise of Ashdown Forest, or to other wooded arms of the High Weald.

It's a land of windmills and castles. At Shipley, King's Windmill is the youngest of the Sussex smock mills. Owned for nearly 50 years by Hilaire Belloc, it ceased grinding corn commercially in 1926, but is now open to the public on set days in summer. As for castles, Bodiam is the quintessential medieval fortress, although it never received or gave a shot or arrow in anger. Solid-looking and romantic, it was built to protect the upper reaches of the River Rother, but is now invaded each summer by National Trust visitors. Herstmonceux Castle is very different, being made of red brick and with a collection of elegant turrets giving a balanced, almost Scottish appearance. Each of these features in walks described in this book.

Although the scenic pleasures to be had on Low Weald walks are not nearly as dramatic as those of the High Weald or the South Downs, they are certainly not without their charm. One wanders across open meadows interspersed with woodland shaws and criss-crossed by narrow lanes. Cattle and sheep graze the pastures, while cereal crops mostly fill the chequerboard fields. Paths lead to farmyards, and from farmyards to lonely cottages that squint across the miles to the blue rise of the Downs. Some of our walks follow the course of meandering rivers, or the route of abandoned railways. Some sneak to the foot of the Downs; some attack their steep north slope to gain a wider view before returning once more to a village base. Some seek out a particular place of interest, like Batemans, for example, while others merely create a circular outing that provides one more aspect of a fascinating county.

THE SOUTH DOWNS

To many Sussex means the South Downs. Perhaps the county's best-loved feature, the Downs offer almost unlimited scope for the walker, all in a setting of considerable charm. Viewed from the north a suave green wall rises out of the Low Weald. At a glance this wall appears to be a narrow one which flanks the coast, but the walker, mounting to its crest, becomes aware that this is not so. For the Downs are surprisingly broad, with hidden, secretive, waterless valleys where the chalk folds and dips into creases, and in places it's several ranges wide before you come to a point where the sea has sliced it clean as a wire through a slab of cheese. The Seven Sisters, for example, reveal a perfect cross-section and a lesson in basic geology - as well as giving a bracing walk along the clifftop above them.

Chalk and flint are the materials of which the Downs are built, scrub its natural growth. The first Neolithic settlers were agriculturalists who tended the high land above the oak forests of Anderida, and it was their flocks which began the age-old process of nibbling that has kept the scrub at bay. Although the numbers of sheep have fallen dramatically, and there are more prairie-like fields of arable land along this range of hills, it is the short, sheep-cropped grass slopes that are characteristic of the "blunt, bow-headed, whale-backed Downs".

In many places they are almost devoid of landmark features and it is not difficult to become disoriented. Where there is no woodland cover the winds blow unhindered, and winter walks can prove to be outings of bitter experience. "The air goes through my coat as if it were gauze," wrote a Victorian naturalist on Ditchling Beacon: "it seems as if the mighty blast rising from that vast plain [the Weald] and glancing up the slope like an arrow ... could lift me up and bear me as it bears a hawk with outspread wings." Conversely, on bright summer days these same unsheltered hills can tax the fittest among us, unless careful thought has been given in advance to suitable clothing and the provision of sufficient liquid refreshment.

On a number of these exposed downland crowns, Iron Age hillforts and other relics of early occupation add interest to the landscape and our wanderings through it. Cissbury Ring is the largest and most impressive at 60 acres, its earthen ramparts still intact some 2300 years after they were first raised. To the north the beeches that marked Chanctonbury Ring were battered by the Great Storm of October 1987, yet those that remain - and others planted with them - still form a notable landmark clearly seen from walks in the Weald far off. Much farther west above Chichester, Bow Hill is topped by a series of Bronze Age burial mounds; to the east Mount Caburn near Glynde housed 70 Celtic families in the third century BC.

The early history of this southern countryside is clearly sketched out for all who are prepared to see it along the South Downs.

But the living history of the Downs is matched by the vibrancy of its natural history: the orchids - early purple, pyramidal, bee,

Dog roses - one of summer's gifts to walkers in Sussex

spider and spotted; the harebells and round-headed rampion ('The Pride of Sussex'); masses of cowslips in the spring, and blood-red poppies in summer - and the trilling of innumerable skylarks, mere specks in an arcing sky. Richard Jefferies took a walk on the Downs above Brighton one wild autumnal day, and wrote of the "larks yonder singing higher still, suspended in the brown light." Is there a walk to be had on the Downs that is without the accompaniment of the skylark? If so, I have yet to experience it. Best of all, walk on a calm summer's day and listen, as W.H. Hudson described it, to "a great number of birds all round the sky pouring out their highest, shrillest notes, so clarified and brightened by distance as to seem like no earthly music."

* * *

NOTES FOR WALKERS

*"The less you carry the more you will see, the less you spend
the more you experience."*
(Stephen Graham 1884-1975)

Walking should not be confined only to the dry summer months
when trees are in full leaf and long, balmy evenings tease you into
staying out late. The countryside has plenty of rewards at all times
of the year and, so long as you're properly attired, in all weathers
too. During research routes described in this book were walked in
every season and in all conditions, and there were no dull days, for
there's as much enjoyment to be gleaned from a crisp winter's walk
as from a stroll on an Indian summer's day; as much magic to be
found in the countryside when autumn mists tease among the trees,
as in the springtime when the meadows, Downs and woodlands
vibrate with new life.

No specialised equipment will be required for tackling these
walks, but it is important to use comfortable footwear, and clothing
suitable for the season that is flexible enough to take account of
changing weather. What you wear should protect you against high
or tangled vegetation, as well as damp crops after rain. For summer
walking, shorts may be adequate on most footpaths, but bear in
mind that brambles and nettles often stray across infrequently-used
paths. Inexpensive overtrousers (preferably with a zipped ankle-
gusset to enable them to be pulled on and off without removing
boots) will prove particularly useful.

It might be worth carrying a few plasters in case of blisters, or for
the odd scratch or two. An Ordnance Survey map will be needed in
the unlikely event of your getting lost, and should also give a
broader picture of the countryside you're walking through than
may be gained from the sketch maps included within these pages.
Details of specific sheets required are provided at the head of each
walk described. I've also noted the availability of refreshments on
each walk. Most of these are to be found at country pubs, although
I must stress that I have no personal experience of any of those
mentioned, so no endorsement is intended. (I prefer to chew an
apple beneath a tree with a view, than sit in a smoky pub!) Should

you plan to stop at a wayside pub or café, please be considerate if your footwear is muddy and either leave your boots in the porch, or cover them with plastic bags.

It is assumed that anyone out for a walk in the countryside will be a lover of that countryside and treat it with due respect. Unfortunately one still comes across pieces of litter where only walkers go. Please be careful not to leave litter, and help in making the countryside more attractive for all by removing any you find. A plastic bag is useful for carrying rubbish away. Maybe then walkers will shame those few farmers who leave fertiliser bags snagged in hedgerows and ditches, and items of once-expensive machinery rusting in a field.

Remember that most paths cross private farmland and estates, but a public right of way is part of the Queen's highway and is subject to the same protection in law as other highways. However, footpaths may not always be abundantly clear on the ground, in which case I trust that directions given in this guidebook will enable you to follow the correct route without difficulty. Where paths lead through growing crops (hay is a crop too), please walk in single file and avoid trespassing. Treat fields of long grass as you would those of ripening wheat, and use stiles or gates where provided to cross hedges, fences and walls, and after use refasten gates found closed.

Crops and animals are a farmer's livelihood and should be left undisturbed. Sheep will be encountered on a number of these walks, and where they are, please keep dogs under control - especially when ewes are in lamb. Farmers have a right to shoot any dogs found worrying livestock.

USING THE GUIDE
Maps:
Sketch maps that accompany each walk described have been produced to give an overview of the route, but are no real substitute for Ordnance Survey maps which obviously provide more accurate detail of the area. At the head of each walk a note of the OS map which covers that route is given. In each case this is from the new Explorer series at a scale of 1:25,000 ($2^{1}/_{2}$" = 1 mile). These give plenty of local detail, including field boundaries, although these may not be 100% accurate due to agricultural changes made since the last survey.

Explorer maps have been brought in to replace the old green-covered Pathfinder sheets, and as they cover a larger area than the Pathfinders, and seem to be printed on more durable paper, they represent very good value. My only quibble is that they cover such a large area that they become almost unmanageable. At first only those maps that covered 'popular' tourist areas such as Ashdown Forest and the South Downs were produced in the Explorer series, but as the whole country is now being covered, sheet numbering for the first three maps has been changed. So it is that you will find references to Explorer 135 (18) 'Ashdown Forest' - 122 (17) 'South Downs Way, Steyning to Newhaven' and 123 (16) 'South Downs Way, Newhaven to Eastbourne' - the bracketed number referring to the first printing of these sheets.

Grid references are frequently quoted to enable you to locate a given position on the OS map, each one of which is divided into a series of vertical and horizontal lines to create a 'grid' (the British National Grid). These lines are provided with a number which is quoted at the top, bottom and sides of each sheet. Numbers increase from left to right for vertical lines (known as 'eastings'), and from top to bottom for horizontal lines ('northings').

To identify an exact point on the map from a given grid reference, take the first two digits from the six-figure number quoted. These refer to the 'eastings' line on the OS map. The third digit is estimated in tenths of the square moving eastwards from that line. Next, take the fourth and fifth digits referring to the 'northings' line, and then the final digit estimating the number of tenths of the square reading up the sheet.

Times and Distances:

Distances quoted in the text, although measured on the OS map, are approximations only, but may be considered reasonably accurate. Note that heights quoted on OS maps are in metres, not in feet, and that grid lines are spaced one kilometre apart.

Allow 2-2$\frac{1}{2}$ miles per hour for your walk, without prolonged stops. Reckon on walking a little slower after wet weather when conditions may be heavy underfoot. When accompanied by children or inexperienced walkers - or indeed, when walking in a group - allow extra time.

Please note: a programme of guided walks is organised during the winter months by both County Councils. These can be very useful for those who are not regular walkers, as well as those who prefer to walk in the company of others. Write to East or West Sussex County Council for details. (The addresses are in Appendix A)

Transport and Car Parking:
It is not practical to give details of all bus and train services in Sussex, since they may change during the period this guidebook is in print. However, an indication is provided of some routes at the head of specific walk details.

The Sussex rail network is operated by Connex South Central. For information on train times and fares, ask at your local staffed station, or call National Rail Enquiries on 0345 484950. (24 hour service.)

For information on public transport in West Sussex call 0345 959099.

For information on public transport in East Sussex call 01273 474747 (Mon to Fri).

If you must use your own transport to reach the start of a walk, the location of suitable car parks is included at the head of route details. However, where there is no official parking facility available, please park sensibly and with due consideration for local residents and farm vehicles, making sure you do not cause an obstruction. If you park near a church, please avoid service times. Do not leave valuables in your vehicle, and be sure to lock your car before setting out on your walk.

*   *   *

Finally, please observe -

The Country Code:

1: Enjoy the countryside and respect its life and work.
2: Guard against all risk of fire.
3: Fasten all gates.
4: Keep dogs under close control.
5: Keep to public paths across farmland.
6: Use gates and stiles to cross fences, hedges and walls.
7: Leave livestock, crops and machinery alone.
8: Take litter home.
9: Help to keep all water clean.
10: Protect wildlife, plants and trees.
11: Take special care on country roads.
12: Make no unnecessary noise.

It was Octavia Hill, that indomitable Victorian champion of the countryside and co-founder of the National Trust, whose words sum up the spirit of the Country Code:

> "Let the grass growing for hay be respected, let the primrose roots be left in their loveliness in the hedges, the birds unmolested and the gates shut. If those who frequented country places would consider those who live there, they would better deserve, and more often retain, the rights and privileges they enjoy."

*   *   *

THE WALKS

WALK 1
Groombridge - Ball's Green - Hartfield - Groombridge

Distance:	9½ miles (or 6½ miles route A, 7½ miles route B options)
Map:	OS Explorer 135 (18) 'Ashdown Forest' 1:25,000
Start:	Groombridge Post Office (Grid ref: 531374)
Access:	Groombridge lies 1¼ miles south of A264 East Grinstead-Tunbridge Wells road, and 4½ miles north of Crowborough; reached by bus from Tunbridge Wells.
Parking:	Public car park opposite Post Office (Grid ref: 532374)
Refreshments:	Pubs in Groombridge, Withyham and Hartfield

The very essence of the High Weald is represented on this walk, by a constant delight of rolling wooded hills with neat coombes and valleys flowing between. The two villages at either end (Groombridge and Hartfield) have attractions of their own; the first of which is unequally shared with Kent, the second with its neat cottages being at the heart of Winnie the Pooh country, for A. A. Milne lived there and drew local landscapes into his children's books. As for the walk itself, this makes a very fine outing - well-waymarked, clear paths, good views and lots of interest throughout. For those who might be daunted by prospects of a 9½ mile walk, two shorter options are offered from the hamlets of Ball's Green (option A - 6½ miles) and Withyham (option B - 7½ miles).

*   *   *

The walk begins along Corseley Road which starts by Groombridge Post Office opposite the car park. Rising gently southward the road leads past the church of St Thomas the Apostle, soon after which it curves right, and a little later bends sharply left and slopes downhill. At the foot of the slope, having left houses behind, cross a stream and immediately turn right on a path signposted to Motts Mill. This is the Sussex Border Path (1). (Grid ref: 529365)

    Cross a field and pass beneath the Edenbridge-Uckfield railway line. Emerging into a large field the path forks on the left. Of the two options take the right-hand path which rises through the field towards a clump of trees, passing just to the right of a World War II

MAP 1

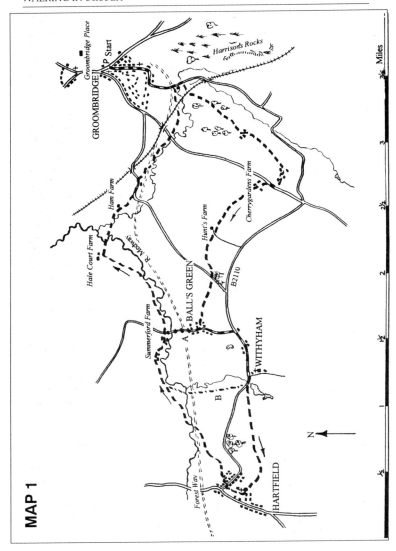

Groombridge Place
P Start
GROOMBRIDGE
Harrisons Rocks
Ham Farm
Hale Court Farm
R. Medway
Summerford Farm
A
BALL'S GREEN
Hunt's Farm
Cherrygardens Farm
B2110
B
WITHYHAM
Forest Way
HARTFIELD
N
Miles

pillbox tucked into the slope. Near the crown of the hill the path goes alongside a small woodland shaw with Sherlock's Farm seen ahead. Keeping to the left of the farm go between some barns then veer left on a track. The track leads along the top edge of fields overlooking a valley watered by the Mottsmill Stream, comes to a crossing path where you continue ahead until, about 700 yards from the farm, you reach a row of cottages on the right of the track. Just beyond these another house stands on the left with a footpath opposite. Bear right here among trees and then along the left-hand end of a long field. After passing a cottage the path leads onto its drive which you follow to a road, the B2188. (Grid ref: 516354)

Turn right and 100 yards later go left into the car park of Cherrygardens Farm where you bear half-right, soon passing along the left-hand side of the farm. The way now goes ahead along the edge of several fields and an orchard, with lovely views encompassing the border country of High Weald ridges of East Sussex and Kent, the shallow valley of the young Medway cutting north between them. The red brick Hunt's Farm stands alone with an uninterrupted panorama to enjoy. Our path crosses its drive and goes ahead over a meadow with that panorama unfolding before you; a peaceful landscape of green wood-crowned hills, neat vales, and patchwork fields outlined with hedgerows and lines of trees, and dotted with the white tips of oasthouses. At the far side of the meadow cross a stile and walk down the edge of a sloping field making for the bottom left-hand corner beside a coppiced woodland crowded with bluebells in spring.

Over the B2110 road enter another field and cross its top left-hand corner to a stile leading into the next field. The path leads directly ahead over this to gain the hamlet of Ball's Green through the edge of Jackass Shaw. Walk along a residential street and come to a crossing road. (Grid ref: 499363) Here is the first opportunity to short-cut the walk and return to Groombridge via Route A.

Route A: Bear right on this road and follow it for 500 yards. Just after crossing the infant River Medway you come to the buildings of Summerford Farm. Immediately opposite the entrance to these, on the right of the road, a footpath sign indicates the route of the Wealdway. Here you rejoin the Main Walk (at Grid ref: 499367) as described later.

Main Walk contd: Turn left along this road until coming to a T junction opposite the half-timbered Duckings Farm. Bear right along the B2110; there is pavement almost as far as the driveway to Withyham Church. At Withyham pass The Dorset Arms pub, and when the pavement ends continue with care alongside the road, passing the driveway to Withyham Church (2) on the left, then a pond. Just beyond this the road curves to the right where there's a second short-cut option. (Grid ref: 493357)

> **Route B:** On the right of the road follow the path of the Wealdway (signposted) across two fields to reach the River Medway. Over this the way soon rejoins the Main Walk (at Grid ref: 493366) as described later.

Main Walk contd: Cross a stile on the left of the road and walk through the middle of a field making for the left side of a woodland. Beyond this the spire of Hartfield Church can be seen ahead. On reaching the far corner go through a gateway into the next field and maintain direction. The path is joined by another as you approach a stile. Crossing the stile walk along the right-hand side of a field and come to another stile beside a field gate. Continue along the right-hand side of the next field until the path leads onto a drive by Hartfield Church. Turn left until reaching the main entrance to the churchyard by a half-timbered cottage whose upper storey projects over the entrance as an archway. The centre of Hartfield (3) lies just ahead.

Note: For refreshments continue a short way down the drive beside attractive half-timbered or weatherboarded cottages to reach The Anchor pub. Just beyond this runs the main street in which there's The Hay Waggon (bear left) and a shop. Hartfield village is certainly worth a short visit.

Go through the churchyard keeping to the left-hand path and exit onto a driveway by the village Primary School. This leads to a meadow with a footpath cutting through it. Follow this path to the B2110. Turn right, then almost immediately cross the road into Castlefields, a residential street. This leads into Motte Field, a street leading off to the right. Just after passing a parking area with garages, bear left on a tarmac path along the back of some houses, then over a stile into a rough meadow, clearly the site of a one-time fortification - a large earthen mound with sunken grass surround that once contained a moat. The way leads to the right, crosses a minor stream and through a gateway into the bottom edge of a field. Another stile just ahead leads into a sloping field where the path follows the bottom left-hand boundary. Enter the next field and a third of the way along its left-hand edge go through a gateway and bear half-right towards the far corner where you come to the former Forest Row to Groombridge railway line, whose course has been adopted as the Forest Way Country Park (4) - a popular bridleway with cyclists and for family outings. (Grid ref: 487364)

Cross the Forest Way (an easy alternative is to follow this to the right as far as the minor road just below Groombridge), then by footbridge over the infant Medway (5). The path now goes ahead and round the right-hand boundary of a field beside trees hiding a pond. The path forks. Continue to the right alongside the woodland shaw and beyond this along the left-hand edge of a meadow with three oasthouses seen ahead. The route is obvious. It leads through a small sloping woodland and joins the Wealdway (6) with a path coming from the right. This is the path adopted by **Route B** from Withyham. (Grid ref: 493366)

Continue ahead, soon coming to the converted Summerford Barn. Walk along the tarmac drive, pass above three oasthouses (now a fine dwelling) seen earlier, and keeping left continue past a whole series of one-time farm buildings now converted into houses, to reach a country road at the entrance to Summerford Farm. This is where the walk is joined by **Route A** from Ball's Green. (Grid ref: 499367)

Cross the road and over a stile into a meadow, still on the route of the Wealdway. (Signpost to Ham Farm) The path leads through a series of meadows and a small woodland, and draws near to Hale Court Farm. At a crossing footpath bear right diagonally across a field. Ahead can be seen the chapel at Burrswood, a Christian centre for medical and spiritual care, on the outskirts of Groombridge. Over the Medway the path maintains direction to a feeder stream where the Wealdway breaks off to the left. Leave it here and continue ahead to Ham Farm, beyond which you reach the B2110 once more. (Grid ref: 515370)

Bear left, and just after passing houses on the right (not shown on the OS map) the road curves left. Over a stile on the right walk across to the embankment carrying the former railway, cross the Forest Way once more and descend into a meadow cut by a small stream. Bear left and follow the stream to the B2188 road. Head to the left for about 80 yards, then take another path on the right (the Sussex Border Path again). About 100 yards from the far end of the field go left beneath the Edenbridge-Uckfield railway line, then half-right across a meadow to Corseley Road (Grid ref: 529366), along which the walk began. Turn left and walk into Groombridge.

Items of interest:

1: The Sussex Border Path as its name suggests, is a long-distance footpath of about 150 miles which traces the county boundary as far as possible. The normal start is at Emsworth on the Hampshire border, with the finish at Rye. See *The Sussex Border Path* by Ben Perkins and Aeneas Mackintosh (Ben Perkins, 11 Old London Road, Brighton BN1 8XR). A shorter version makes a north-south route between East Grinstead and Brighton, by following the present border between East and West Sussex.

2: Withyham Church was originally built in the 14th century, but was extensively rebuilt in 1672 after being badly damaged by lightning in 1663. According to an eye-witness, the lightning 'came in at the steeple, melted the bells, and went up the chancel, where it tore the monuments of the Dorsets to pieces.' Fifteen generations of the Sackville family (of Knole, Sevenoaks) lie in the family vault in the Sackville Chapel. Of the many memorials is a simple tablet dedicated to the writer, Victoria (Vita) Sackville-West, who died in 1962. It reads: 'V. Sackville-West C.H., poet.' The village of Withyham was mentioned in the Domesday Book of 1086, and four of the farms named then still exist - Ham Farm, Hendal Farm, Hale Court Farm and Grubbs Farm, the latter renamed Friars Gate Farm.

3: Hartfield is an attractive village nestling below the northern slopes of Ashdown Forest, and its name (meaning 'open land where the harts [or deer] graze') clearly shows its link with the former royal hunting ground of Ashdown Forest. The centre of the village consists of a number of white weatherboarded cottages, and with half-timbered buildings on the road leading to the church. In 1925 A.A. Milne bought Cotchford Farm south of the village (the house was later bought by Rolling Stone, Brian Jones, who died there), and wove local scenes into his *Winnie the Pooh* stories. A shop in the main street ('Pooh Corner') makes the most of Milne characters.

4: The Forest Way is a linear Country Park developed along the 9 mile trackbed of the dismantled East Grinstead-Groombridge branch line. Bought by East Sussex County Council in 1971, it was designated a Country Park three years later.

5: The River Medway is generally known as Kent's major waterway, although it has several of its sources here in East Sussex. It forms the Sussex-Kent border north-west of Groombridge and spills into the Thames Estuary at Sheerness, 70 miles from its birth. See *Medway Valley Walk* by Kev Reynolds (Kent County Council).

6: The Wealdway is a long-distance route that begins on the banks of the Thames at Gravesend, and ends 82 miles later on Beachy Head after crossing the North Downs, various High Weald ridges, Ashdown Forest and, last of all, the South Downs. See *The Wealdway & The Vanguard Way* by Kev Reynolds (Cicerone Press).

WALK 2
Eridge Station - Groombridge - Eridge Station

Distance:	8 miles (or 6$^{1}/_{2}$ miles route A option)
Map:	OS Explorer 135 (18) 'Ashdown Forest' 1:25,000
Start:	Eridge Railway Station (Grid ref: 542345)
Access:	By train on the London Victoria-Oxted-Uckfield line. By bus from Tunbridge Wells or Crowborough. By road: A26, Tunbridge Wells-Crowborough.
Parking:	At the station.
Refreshments:	None en route, but pubs & shops in Groombridge ($^{1}/_{2}$ mile), and pub near Eridge Station.

Typical of the High Weald country of East Sussex, this walk enjoys a generously wooded landscape, as a glance at the Ordnance Survey map will

MAP 2

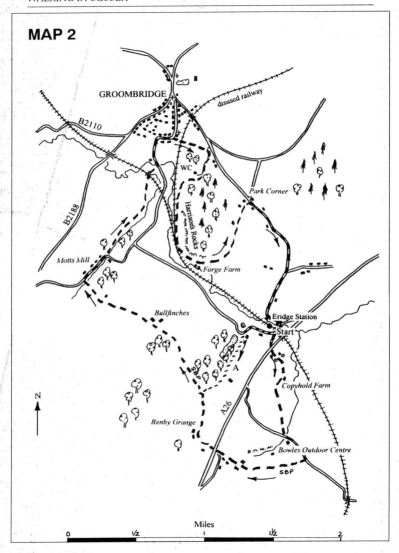

GROOMBRIDGE

disused railway

B2110

WC

Park Corner

B2188

Harrison's Rocks

Motts Mill

Forge Farm

Bullfinches

Eridge Station

Start

A

Copyhold Farm

N

Renby Grange

A26

Bowles Outdoor Centre

SBP

Miles

0   ½   1   1½   2

Harrison's Rocks, Mecca for climbers throughout southern England *(Walk 2)*
Walkers on the Forest Way near Hartfield *(Walk 8)*

Ashdown Forest blazes purple in the summer *(Walk 10)*
Nutley Mill, the oldest working windmill in Sussex *(Walk 11)*

testify. But it also has plenty of open countryside too, some of it stumped with outcrops of sandstone, or cut by innocent streams that flow north towards the Medway. One of the highlights is the long line of Harrison's Rocks south of Groombridge. This is a rock climber's playground on the edge of Birchden Wood, while to the south of Eridge Station is located Bowles Outdoor Pursuits Centre with its own sandstone crags emblazoned with rhododendrons in early summer.

*   *   *

Come out of Eridge Station and turn right. In a few paces Forge Road breaks off to the right. Readers who plan to tackle the shorter (6¹⁄₂ mile) Route A, should follow directions below.

> **Route A:** Walk along Forge Road. In a short distance the road makes a sharp left-hand bend, then curves right near a pond. Leave the road here and walk up a stony drive on the left. Just after passing Hamsell Lake House go ahead on a path along the edge of woodland. (Hamsell Lake may just be glimpsed through the trees to the right.) Arriving at the lower corner of a large field, walk along its right-hand edge and when the woodland cuts back to the right, maintain direction to gain a track near the large barns of Renby Farm. Continue ahead, once more with the woodland on your right. When the wood ends the track curves right (the Sussex Border Path) and here you join the main route at Grid ref: 534336.

Main Walk contd: Ignoring Forge Road continue to the A26, cross with care and turn right for a few paces, then go left by a bus stop on a narrow drive which leads to Hamsell Farm. After passing a house curve right on a track leading to a gate. Through this wander ahead along the right-hand boundary of a field to another field gate. Go through this and along the drive of Copyhold Farm. About 100 yards beyond the farm cross a large field on the left. At the far side turn left on Sandhill Lane and very shortly pass the entrance to Bowles Outdoor Centre. (Grid ref: 544332)

Continue uphill and at the top of the rise turn right on a track, joining the Sussex Border Path (1). Cross a stile and walk along the right-hand edge of a field, soon gaining views off to the right to a rim of sandstone rocks used for climbing courses run by Bowles Outdoor Centre. Enter a second field and go round the broad left-hand headland. This leads to some barns at Rocks Farm. Skirt round the left-hand side of these, then bear right on a drive between the barns and a house. The drive passes one or two more houses and comes to a narrow road. Bear right on a tarmac footpath and cross the A26 once more. On the west side of the road a continuing footpath brings you to another narrow road where you turn left along a tree-lined track/drive beside the drive to Green Loanings. (Grid ref: 535331)

When the track/drive forks continue straight ahead, sloping downhill on a sunken way between trees, so to reach Little Renby and Renby Grange. Continue on the drive, which is now flanked on the right by a rhododendron hedge, and about 100 yards beyond Renby Grange cross a stile on the left. In a few paces the path cuts into a woodland shaw; a splendid sunken trail among beech and oak soaring from steep banks. When the sunken section ends maintain direction on a broad grass path that comes to a junction of tracks (Grid ref: 534336), joined by **Route A**.

Bear left (still on the Sussex Border Path) on a track beside a wood. At the foot of the slope come to a junction of paths. Cross a stile ahead to the right and walk up through the centre of a sloping field to a group of trees. Pass along the left-hand side of these and ahead through another field to a path junction. Maintain direction alongside more woodland, cross an open section of field and come to Marchant Wood. With this to your left keep ahead, go over a crossing track and a footbridge, then through a long field towards Bullfinches. Pass to the left of tennis courts, cross a stile (lovely views behind) and continue towards a farm. (Grid ref: 526346)

The path enters a field to the left of the farm and maintains direction through a series of fields until coming to a narrow drive leading to a white house on the right. Continue ahead through another field, then over a stile go down a slope beside Rocks Wood. At the bottom corner another stile and a footbridge beyond takes the path into trees and scrub where you climb quite steeply to a narrow lane at Motts Mill. Bear right. After passing a few cottages the lane curves to the right at the foot of a slope. Leave it here and walk ahead on a path into trees alongside Mottsmill Stream. Ignore alternative paths cutting off to the left, and wander ahead through woods

Cottages at Motts Mill

(bluebells in spring) until you emerge into a long, narrow meadow. Maintain direction, but at the far end cross a stile and go up the slope half-left to another stile. This leads into a large field with Groombridge (2) seen in the distance ahead. The footpath cuts through the field, then passes beneath a railway line. Cross the rough field beyond and come onto a country road where you bear left. (Grid ref: 529365)

Passing a water treatment works, walk up the road for about a third of a mile. Near the head of the slope the road makes a sharp right-hand bend among houses, and soon after curves left. At this second bend (Grid ref: 531368) take a path on the right which goes alongside the boundary of St Thomas CE Primary School. (*Note:* If refreshments are needed, remain on the road for almost ¹/₂ mile, and in the middle of Groombridge you'll find pubs and shops.) At the end of the school boundary cross the now disused Tunbridge Wells-Eridge branch railway line (closed 1985) by a footbridge, and maintain direction across a field, following the route of the High Weald Walk (3). On coming to a driveway turn right. Just before it curves left, cut left on a footpath among trees. This slopes downhill

35

and crosses the drive to a broad stony path by the side of the car park for Harrison's Rocks. (There's a public toilet within this car park.) (Grid ref: 534364)

The path comes to a field gate and you continue ahead on a track curving left beside the disused railway line. Reach an open area with Harrison's Rocks (4) seen off to the left. On the right the disused railway line is soon joined by the working line that runs through Eridge Station. At the end of the open section of pastureland the track re-enters woodland and eventually arrives at another field gate by the tile-hung house named Birchden Forge. Walk along its drive, past an attractive converted oasthouse and another house beyond, then maintain direction on a footpath. (Grid ref: 533353)

Rising now into Birchden Wood the path approaches another field gate with a stile beside it. Just before reaching this, note the oak tree on the right which has grown upon a bank. The bank has crumbled away in places, to create a small hollow 'cave' immediately beneath the upright trunk. Over the stile the path forks. Continue ahead on the right branch and the way soon becomes a hedge-lined track with big views off to the right and behind. The track leads to a farm drive, at the far end of which you come to a junction of country lanes at Park Corner. (Grid ref: 539360) Turn right and follow the lane for $1^{1}/_{4}$ miles back to Eridge Station.

Items of interest:

1: The Sussex Border Path makes a circuit of the county on rights of way, drawing close to the boundaries of Hampshire, Surrey and Kent, but with a shorter version which follows the East and West Sussex border from East Grinstead to Brighton. (See *The Sussex Border Path* by Ben Perkins and Aeneas Mackintosh.)

2: Groombridge straddles the borders of Kent and East Sussex. Sussex boasts the larger portion, but the Kentish part consists of an attractive group of cottages and a pub lining a triangular green on a slope. Groombridge Place dates from the late 17th century. It has a moat, a lake, and gardens that are open to the public.

3: The High Weald Walk makes a $27^{1}/_{2}$ mile circuit through country-side around Tunbridge Wells. The walk was developed by the Kent High Weald Project and High Weald Conservation Project (East

Sussex) in the early 1990s, and an illustrated guide to the route was written by Bea Cowan. (See *High Weald Walk* by Bea Cowan, Kent County Council.)

4: Harrison's Rocks, named after 18th century landowner and firearms manufacturer, William Harrison, were the first in Britain to be owned by climbers themselves through the British Mountaineering Council. The sandstone outcrop is 40ft high in places, and has proved popular with adepts and beginners alike who, for decades, have flocked there at weekends and throughout the summer holidays. Several youth groups use the facilities to learn climbing skills. Other outcrops in this corner of the High Weald include High Rocks on the outskirts of Tunbridge Wells, Eridge Rocks near Eridge Green, and those at Bowles Outdoor Centre visited near the start of the walk.

WALK 3
Wadhurst Station - Earlye Farm - Wadhurst Station

Distance:	5½ miles (or 5 miles route A option)
Maps:	OS Explorer 136 'The Weald' 1:25,000
Start:	Wadhurst Railway Station (Grid ref: 622330)
Access:	By train on the London-West St Leonards line; by road via B2099 1½ miles north-west of Wadhurst.
Parking:	At the station.
Refreshments:	Two pubs near Wadhurst Station.

This is quite a strenuous, hilly walk that climbs in and out of the wooded ghylls that are very much a feature of this part of the High Weald. There are high meadows, farms, dense woodlands and deep valleys through which modest streams meander. It is a very peaceful, varied countryside with plenty to enjoy. In springtime most of the woodland sections are carpeted with bluebells and/or wild garlic; in early summer rhododendrons blaze among gardens, while there are many splendid specimen trees to admire.

*   *   *

On leaving Wadhurst Station bear left along the B2099 for about 500 yards, then turn left into Faircrouch Lane (direction Tidebrook).

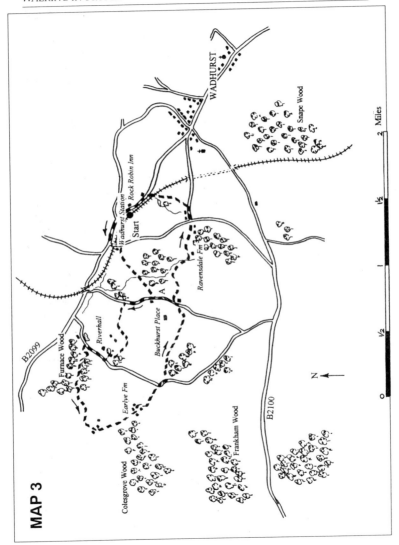

MAP 3

Snape Wood

WADHURST

Rock Robin Inn

Wadhurst Station

Start

Ravensdale Fm

Riverhall

Buckhurst Place

B2009

Furnace Wood

Earlye Fm

Colesgrove Wood

Frankham Wood

B2100

N

0   ½   1   1½   2 Miles

Crossing the railway the lane rises uphill, and immediately beyond the boundary fence of a civic amenity site, you leave it and turning right find a gate into a field. Wander across the field veering slightly left to a stile in the opposite hedgerow. Cross this and follow the left-hand boundary which soon slopes downhill, but on coming to a gate, enter the adjacent field on the left and then aim for the bottom left-hand corner where two streams converge. Cross these and walk up a field towards its top left-hand corner. Pass through a gateway, continue towards a white weatherboarded house, and come onto a narrow lane opposite Groomden Farm. (Grid ref: 612327)

Turn right. Wandering down the lane pass Hillyfields Farm, and some way beyond this come to a timber-framed house tucked among trees. This is called Robins Wood. A few paces before reaching it, leave the lane and cross a stile half-hidden in the left-hand hedge. Go up the right-hand boundary of a sloping field, pass through a gap on the far side and maintain direction through the next field. On coming to a stile bear half-left down through a small meadow in which there's a shed, and at the bottom left-hand corner go through another hedgerow gap, maintain direction over a ditch, then turn half-right. The path leads to a gateway and you then continue down to the bottom right-hand corner of the next field. Over a small stream the way leads along the bottom of a slope, passes an isolated tennis court, and going through a boggy area enters woods and turns right. Reaching a narrow stony track, bear left, with the imposing Riverhall seen a short distance away. The track-cum-drive leads directly to a very narrow lane. (Grid ref: 604333)

Once again turn right and soon pass cottages on the left. At the far end of a woodland (unmarked on the OS map) turn left onto a footpath. (150 yards or so further along the lane stands the handsome thatched Mill House.) The path, which can be a little muddy at times, rises gently along the edge of Furnace Wood, then makes a sharp right then left into the wood itself above a stream. When the path divides take the lower option, and shortly after walk along the right-hand side of a small pond. Leave the wood through a gate and follow the right-hand boundary of a sloping field. On gaining the top left-hand corner pass through another gate into a second field by two sheds. Pass these to your left and in the next corner go through a field gate and walk along the top edge of the field to gain a driveway. (Grid ref: 595334)

Walk straight ahead to pass a cottage on the left, and when the drive curves right, leave it and use a squeeze stile to enter the field ahead where there are three paths. Bear left and just beyond the next corner go through another squeeze stile and walk down the slope almost beneath power lines. It's a steep slope, and at the bottom you cross a stream by footbridge, then climb steps among trees to another sloping field. At the top of this a barn can be seen, and as you progress up the field towards it, other barns appear. Walk between the barns, then along a track which passes to the right of the tilehung Earlye Farm and goes towards a converted oasthouse. (Grid ref: 598329)

Immediately beyond the oasthouse follow the track to the right and come to two field gates. Go through that on the left and walk ahead on the left-hand side of a field, and at the bottom corner enter woodland on a clear path. Emerging from the wood turn right along a very narrow lane for about 250 yards, then cross a stile on the left into a short field. Across this enter another woodland, and after a few paces cross a footbridge and climb a series of steps to gain another field. Wander up the right-hand edge and at the brow of the hill cross a stile on the right and maintain direction along the left-hand boundary of a large field. On the far side a few low rocks peep above the turf, and just beyond you cross a stile and continue ahead through two fields to gain another narrow lane opposite the entrance to Woodcote. Turn left for about 30 yards. (Grid ref: 611325)

Route A: A slightly shorter return to Wadhurst Station can be achieved by continuing along the lane for a further 350 yards to Groomden Farm, where you take the path on the right which reverses the first section of the outer route. This will save about ¹/₂ mile of walking.

Main Walk contd: A stile on the right gives access to a sloping meadow near the bottom of which another stile takes you into a belt of trees where the path cuts half-left down to a stream. The path then works its way through two low-lying fields divided by a line of trees, then yet another stile in the left-hand fence leads the path alongside a pleasant stream among trees. Water-smoothed rocks offer a way over the stream, and the path continues by following the right-hand edge of a field to a drive opposite the handsome, timber-framed Ravensdale Farm. Bear left along the drive to a junction of lanes. Walk directly ahead along the lane opposite. When it curves to the right bear left on a drive marked Tapsells Lane Farm. On coming to a collection of barns take a footpath along the left-hand side of these to enter woodland. Beyond the woods wander across a field to the far right-hand corner, and through trees cross the railway line where the continuing path will soon bring you to the B2099 opposite the Four Keys pub. Walk down the road to Wadhurst Station.

WALK 4
Mayfield - Wadhurst Park - Mayfield

Distance:	8 miles (or 8¹/₂ miles route A option)
Map:	OS Explorer 136 'The Weald' 1:25,000
Start:	Mayfield Recreation Ground (Grid ref: 588271)
Access:	By bus on the Tunbridge Wells-Heathfield route. Mayfield is located east of A267 about 10 miles south of Tunbridge Wells.
Parking:	Public car park (with toilets) south of the High Street (Grid ref: 587269). Parking also at entrance to recreation ground.
Refreshments:	Pubs, tearoom and shops in Mayfield, otherwise none on route.

This walk explores the quintessential countryside of the High Weald - rolling hills and woodlands, and trim valleys drained by modest meandering streams; on this occasion these streams are tributaries of the Rother. There are no villages or hamlets once we leave Mayfield, but the route passes a number of lovely houses and farms tucked quietly away from the general public gaze. The highlight, however, is Wadhurst Park with its tranquil lake and herds of deer, a huge area of park- and woodland in a fold of hills. Mayfield, where we begin and end, is one of the most attractive of High Weald villages, built upon a ridge with a handsome main street lined with half-timbered, ragstone, tile-hung or weatherboarded buildings, and a one-

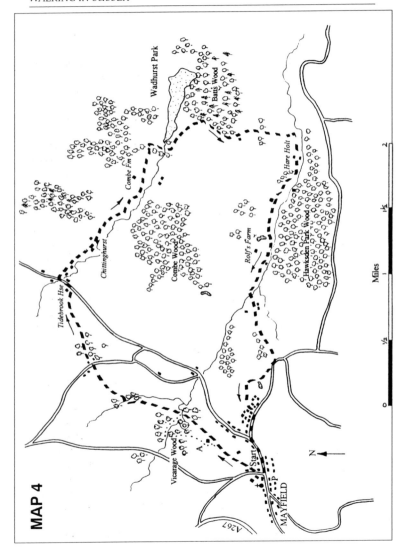

MAP 4

time archbishop's palace standing back behind an impressive Tudor gatehouse.

* * *

The entrance to Mayfield's recreation ground is located between the Scout headquarters and the village memorial hall, beside the road heading north from the eastern end of the High Street. Walk down the path cutting half-left away from the memorial hall, aiming towards the left-hand end of a football pitch. At once there are pleasant views in sight. The path enters a wooded area, crosses a track and then over a stile into a field. Follow the right-hand boundary to a second field. (Grid ref: 591274) Here we have a choice of routes, and although the main walk continues ahead, the alternative is also worth considering.

> **Route A:** Cross the field towards the far left-hand corner, where waymarks and a series of stiles lead a path round the left-hand garden boundary of a converted oasthouse. As you descend a large sloping field beyond the house veer left away from the edge to locate a stile in the bottom boundary, about 100 yards from the field corner. Over this stile you enter Vicarage Wood, cross a small stream and, on the edge of the wood, come to a crossing path and bear right. Soon come to a major path junction. Turn right, in effect returning into the wood alongside a stream. At the next meeting of paths by a concrete footbridge rejoin the Main Walk by crossing the stile on the left. (Grid ref: 595279)

Main Walk contd: Maintain direction along the right-hand edge of a succession of fields going down a slope towards Vicarage Wood, which is entered by some wooden bars fitted across the path. One or two alternative unmarked paths break away from the main route through this wood, but the correct way is obvious. Just before reaching a stream the path forks. Continue across a concrete footbridge and cross a stile into a small field to be rejoined by **Walk A**. (Grid ref: 595279)

Walk up the left-hand edge and through a gap where you continue ahead through the middle of a larger field. Across the slope locate a narrow gap in the opposite boundary hedge, enter a third field and maintain direction. On the hillside to the right

Pennybridge Farm is a major landmark, while ahead stands a small wood. The path goes along its left-hand side, and half-way along the field a marker post indicates the position of a stile which directs the point at which you enter the wood. Crossing an initial ditch, the path swings sharply to the right and crosses a stream by a plank footbridge. Over this turn left at a junction of paths and soon leave the wood. Bear slightly right and wander along the lower, right-hand boundary of a field, and about 100 yards short of the far corner, veer right through a belt of trees, cross another stream and pass through a kissing gate into a sloping meadow. (This appears to be part of a large garden.) Cross to the end of a woodland shaw, then cut directly up the slope aiming a little to the right of a small garage. There you come to a stile giving onto a minor road. (Grid ref: 601290) At this point look back to enjoy a very pleasing view.

Cross the road directly ahead onto a drive, and beyond this continue ahead on a footpath among trees. When this forks take the right branch, still among trees. The path is obvious and leads for some way through a woodland shaw and on a broad grass track, eventually coming to the grounds of Tidebrook House. Enter the grounds over a stile, a few paces beyond which there's a large wooden owl carved from what looks like the trunk of a Scots pine. Shortly before coming to the turreted red-brick house the path has been diverted right, through a gap in a hedge and round the inner boundary of a small orchard, then out to a drive. Turn right and walk up to a minor road. Just before leaving the drive note the dragon perched on the ridge-tile of the lodge on the right. Bear left and walk down the road. At the bottom of the slope the road crosses the Tide Brook stream and curves left. (Grid ref: 612294)

At this point bear right along a drive leading to Chittinghurst. After about a third of a mile the drive forks, with the converted Chittinghurst Barn to the left. Take the right branch, and immediately past the house (Chittinghurst) the drive ends and a hedge-lined track continues. Wander along this until it crosses a minor stream and enters a field through a gate. Cross to the far right-hand corner where you come to a crossing path between gates. Keep ahead along the left-hand edge of the next field, and on entering another field ahead, follow the right-hand boundary, cross a stream dividing two fields and continue to a stile in the opposite boundary. Following the stream (the Tide Brook) you reach a farm drive and bear left for a few paces, then the continuing path breaks off to the right, passes beside a willow tree and into a large field below Combe Farm. The way strikes through the middle of the field, which is divided by a wire fence crossed by yet another stile, and on the far side you go through a belt of trees to a gate in a deer fence surrounding Wadhurst Park. (Grid ref: 628284) Dogs must be kept on a lead.

Walk directly ahead up a slope to a crossing track and there bear right. Wadhurst Park Lake can be seen a short distance to the east. Look for deer as you wander through the parkland. The track slopes down to pass through a gap, then forks. Take the left branch. When the track fades marker posts lead the way across the parkland above the lake, then out by way of a second gate in the deer fence - at which point there's a lovely view across the lake to a luxuriously green rolling landscape. Now the path is fed along the edge of Batt's Wood. Ignore two paths which break away left, and maintain direction. Keep to the left of a small house and come to a field, which you cross to the lower left-hand corner. Go through a woodland area with a pond on the right, and continue through an extensive woodland shaw between fields. At one point the way leads into the right-hand field, but after 30 yards returns to the shaw. At the foot of the slope come to a crossing bridleway. (Grid ref: 629266)

Turn right through more trees and eventually come to the neat garden of Hare Holt. Wander ahead to the drive and pass between the typically Wealden house and an oasthouse. Remain on the drive until it curves slightly left. At this point the continuing bridleway goes ahead alongside a stream. When the bridleway veers left to rejoin the drive by a house, bear right among more trees and enter a field. Maintain direction, then cut through a patch of coppice woodland. Leave this through a gate, and bear left along a track to a white weatherboarded house. (Grid ref: 621269)

Immediately after passing through a gateway by the entrance to the house, veer half-left down a grass slope and through a series of low-lying fields. Eventually come to the outbuildings of Rolf's Farm. Bear right, then a few paces later go round the farm buildings to the left. Immediately past the barns go through the right-hand of two gates and walk ahead alongside a stream. At the end of this field section a stile takes you onto a crossing path by a footbridge. Bear left over the stream and follow a bridleway ahead for nearly half a mile, soon passing a complex of farm buildings on the left. On coming to a broad, sunken track, continue ahead, and gain a road leading to Mayfield. (Grid ref: 601268)

Do not go onto the road, but turn right onto a short track with a footpath sign to Coggins Mill Road. Entering a field follow the left-hand boundary (more fine views to the right), and continue in the same direction in a second field, in the top corner of which cross a stile to a junction of paths and bear left through a dark woodland shaw. Now walk aross the last field and along the bottom of a row of houses. The way leads into a residential street which you cross half right to a hedge-lined path. This takes you onto the road once more where you bear right and walk on into the heart of Mayfield, (1) passing two pubs on the way - first The Rose and Crown, and next The Carpenters Arms.

Items of interest:

1: Mayfield, considered by some as the finest High Weald parish in Sussex, is a prosperous-looking hilltop village with a most attractive main street, and the one-time residence of the Archbishops of Canterbury. This was founded by St Dunstan in the 10th century, but the last to own it was Thomas Cranmer who handed it over to Henry VIII in 1545. The remains of the palace building, restored by Pugin, now form part of a convent, with the Victorian Roman Catholic school of St Leonard's next door. On the south side of the High Street is the half-timbered 14th century Walnut Tree House. Mayfield earned its prosperity as a centre of Wealden iron-working.

WALK 5
Mayfield - Moat Mill Farm - Mayfield

Distance:	4¹/₂ miles
Map:	OS Explorer 135 (18) 'Ashdown Forest' 1:25,000
Start:	Mayfield church (Grid ref: 587270)
Access:	By bus on the Tunbridge Wells-Heathfield route. Mayfield is located east of A267 about 10 miles south of Tunbridge Wells.

Parking: Public car park (with toilets) south of High Street (Grid ref: 587269)

Refreshments: Pubs, tearoom and shops in Mayfield.

There are plenty of good walks to be had from Mayfield, as a glance at the map will testify, and when you gaze over the countryside spreading south of the High Street one senses that this green and welcoming land will not disappoint. On this particular walk a series of meadow, woodland and streamside paths draw together some of the best Wealden landscapes in this corner of Sussex. On top of that a number of delightful buildings add scale to the scenery, and help create an outing of considerable charm.

*   *   *

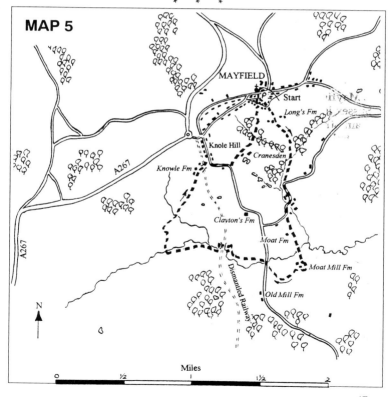

St Dunstan's church, with its graceful spire, overlooks the elegant High Street from the north side. Almost opposite this, to the south, a narrow alleyway slopes away from the High Street between buildings (signed to the Bowling Green) and shortly leads to a lane just west of the public car park. Turn left, then right on a continuing path going downhill at the back of houses, and spilling out at a junction of lanes. Walk ahead to pass Mayfield Bowls Club. The lane ends at a house with a gate marked Strathbourne. Go through this on a footpath which continues beyond the house down a slope, and through scrub with views to wooded hills. Entering woods the path still eases downhill to a stream, then up the opposing slope, out alongside meadows and on to a narrow lane at a sharp bend. (Grid ref: 590259)

Walk directly ahead on the hedge-lined lane, passing a few houses, one of which is a fine converted oasthouse. After this the lane rises uphill, and when it starts to bend to the right, you cross a stile into the left-hand field and bear right. In a short distance cross a second stile among trees into the next field ahead and maintain direction. The way continues through a series of linking fields during which you pass Moat Farm (seen on the right) and, soon after crossing a stream, enter the grounds of Moat Mill Farm. When you reach a small brick building, the path goes round its left-hand side, then forks. Ignore that to the left, and a few paces later bear right over a stile and walk along the left-hand edge of a garden towards a converted oasthouse where you join a drive. Wander along this drive, but soon after it curves right, where it is joined by another drive, cross a stile into the right-hand field. The way cuts through this field, passes just left of a telegraph pole and exits onto a country road by St Dunstan's Bridge. (Grid ref: 588249)

Turn right to cross the bridge, then use a stile to gain entry to the left-hand field. Cross this ahead, and in the centre of the far boundary you'll find another stile. Over this bear slightly right through a gap, then follow the left-hand hedge towards a handsome tile-hung house. As you approach the house a finger post directs the way half-right to a stile by a field gate. This takes you into an orchard, which you cross to a drive. There you bear left, and beyond the house walk through an archway over which a branch line used to carry trains to Heathfield, Horsham and Polegate. Out of the archway turn left, and soon go through a gap into a second field where you bear right. (Grid ref: 582251)

Follow the bottom edge of this sloping field and at the far corner pass into the next field ahead. Maintain direction to a third field, but about 60 yards later cross a footbridge on your right. (There's a junction of paths here.) Walk alongside the right-hand boundary and at the top corner cross a concrete farm road and continue ahead. In the distance the white-painted windmill on Argos Hill can be seen (1). About 20 yards from a small woodland, go through a gate on the right and walk down a slope with Knowle Farm seen on the opposite slope ahead. At the foot of the slope a footbridge carries the path over a stream among trees, beyond which you rise steadily through two sloping meadows linked by a stile. At the top of the second of these, go through a gate just left of farm buildings. Here you come onto a track/drive which winds uphill past barns and stables to join a crossing drive serving Knowle Farm. A lovely view is gained here across a plunging valley to the windmill again. Turn right, cross a bridge over a deep cutting through which the abandoned railway once travelled, and come onto a country road at Knole Hill. (Grid ref: 581262)

Turn right along the road (Newick Lane) which soon curves downhill. Towards the foot of the slope, just after rounding a right-hand bend, cut back left on a fenced footpath alongside a wood. Through some trees continue along the bottom of a sloping meadow, pass through a gap into the next meadow ahead and go gently uphill beside a barn. On reaching the top corner come to a crossing drive. Cross this slightly right and up some stone steps into another field with Mayfield (2) seen ahead. Walk ahead (a drive to the right) and at the far corner enter woods and plunge downhill to cross another stream by a plank footbridge. Emerge from the woods and wander up a sloping meadow divided into paddocks, at the top of which a narrow continuing footpath leads between houses. On coming to a very narrow lane bear left and about 30 yards later turn right on a tarmac footpath which crosses another narrow lane and continues into Mayfield High Street where the walk began.

Items of interest:

1: Argos Hill Windmill is a post mill converted to a museum, but it is only infrequently open to the public.

2: Mayfield in the early 18th century was home to a notorious gang of smugglers, whose leader was Gabriel Tomkins, alias Kitt Jarvis or Joseph Rawlins. The Mayfield gang would land contraband goods along the coast between Hastings and Seaford, and had depots not only in Mayfield, but also at Horsham and West Chiltington. After a whole series of narrow escapes in a career worthy of schoolboy fiction, Tomkins was hanged as a highwayman in 1745.

WALK 6
Hartfield - Marsh Green - Hartfield

Distance:	7¹/₂ miles (or 5¹/₂ miles route A, 7 miles route B options)
Map:	OS Explorer 135 (18) 'Ashdown Forest' 1:25,000
Start:	Hartfield Parish Church (Grid ref: 479357)
Access:	By B2110, 4 miles east of Forest Row, or via B2188/B2110, 6 miles north-west of Crowborough.
Parking:	With discretion in the village
Refreshments:	None on the walk, but pubs in Hartfield.

Hartfield is an attractive village of white weatherboarded cottages lying on the north side of Ashdown Forest. Its best-known former resident was A.A. Milne, creator of the Winnie the Pooh books, who wrote many of the local landscape features into his stories. This circular walk visits Milne's 'Hundred Acre Wood' (Five Hundred Acre Wood in reality), while option A crosses the so-called 'Poohsticks Bridge' that is known far and wide. It's a delightful walk whose footpaths lead to several fine views, as well as delightful sections of woodland that are attractive all year round.

*   *   *

From the main street walk along the drive which passes the south side of Hartfield's church, cross a stile on the right and follow the left-hand boundary of a meadow to a field gate with a stile beside it. Over this maintain direction along the edge of a second field, on the far side of which you enter a large open field with two paths cutting through it. Take the right-hand of these; in effect continuing ahead to the bottom far corner. Pass through a gateway between

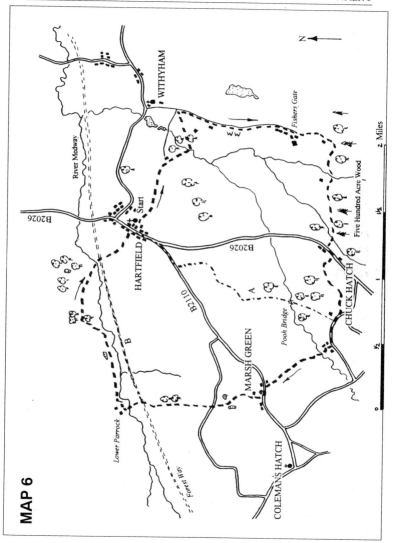

MAP 6

woodland shaws and veer right. Withyham church can be seen off to the left. In a few paces go through another gateway and bear left, soon passing alongside Forstal Farm. (Grid ref: 487354)

Cross a bridge over a stream (a tributary of the Medway) and bear left to walk across a partially enclosed meadow, in the top corner of which a path continues ahead through a patch of woodland. Emerging from the trees come into a sloping meadow and cross aiming for the top corner where a stile brings you onto a narrow private road where you join the route of the Wealdway (1). (Grid ref: 493353)

Turn right and follow the road for one mile, as far as the entrance gateway to Fisher's Gate. Along the way pass a handsome thatched house (Thatchers) set among tall Scots pines, beyond which lies heavily-wooded rolling countryside, with Ashdown Forest rising directly ahead. On coming to the gateway to Fisher's Gate our path breaks off to the left, enclosed by fences leading to Five Hundred Acre Wood (2). On reaching a junction of drives at the entrance to the wood, continue ahead, still following Wealdway signs. This curves to the right and passes a house. The drive forks and we continue along the right-hand branch. Remain on the surfaced drive as far as the gateway to Kovacs Lodge. Now go ahead on a track beside a deer fence. When the Wealdway cuts left at a junction, we continue ahead, with meadows to the right and Ashdown Forest on the left. Soon enter woods (predominantly beech), cross a stream and rise gently along what soon becomes a sunken track leading to the B2026 road opposite houses. (Grid ref: 477335)

Bear left for about 160 yards, then cross a stile on the right and walk across a meadow used for exercising horses. On the far side come to a farm track. Over this another stile gives access to an open field through which a footpath crosses to the far corner on the edge of Posingford Wood. Enter the woods where the path leads to a small enclosed meadow which you cross to a gateway and a stone footpath marker. Continue ahead, and in a few paces bear right at a broad, well-trodden crossing path. On reaching a country road walk ahead along it, and in a few paces a surfaced bridleway by a barn cuts off to the right to Poohsticks Bridge. This is the route of option A. (Grid ref: 468334)

Route A: Walk along this bridleway down a slope and into woodland leading directly to Poohsticks Bridge - a very popular site for adults as well as children, who gather here to play Poohsticks! Visitors from as far afield as Japan are often seen here. Continue beyond the bridge and up the slope to a narrow lane. When this forks soon after take the left branch. As it curves leftward, cross a stile on the right and follow the left-hand boundary of a meadow until coming to another stile which now takes the path up a sloping field. On the way up this slope take a moment to enjoy the backward view to Ashdown Forest. On the crown of the hill come onto a drive opposite a tile-hung house, and there turn right. Over a stile enter a hilltop meadow and wander along its left-hand boundary, passing in front of a large white house. (Magnificent views off to the right.) Beyond the house turn left and in a corner where there's a junction of paths, cross a stile and walk down the slope beyond, now with fine views north to the far distant Greensand Ridge. At the foot of the slope come to the B2110 (Grid ref: 474353). Cross with care, bear right and follow the road down to Hartfield. 'Pooh Corner' (3) is passed soon after entering the village.

Main Walk contd: Wander along the road for another 350 yards, and just before it curves sharply to the left, bear right on a driveway between the Old School House and Hartswood. This is Marsh Green. Beyond the houses a footpath continues ahead, crosses a stream on a footbridge and enters a sloping meadow. Walk through this to its top far corner, from where lovely views are to be had back to the rise of Ashdown Forest, all heather-covered slopes and stands of pine. Over a stile enter another meadow where there are two paths. Ours is the left-hand option, cutting along the boundary to a field gate giving access to another meadow with Fincham Farm ahead. Waymarks direct the path along the right-hand side of tennis courts and a pond, before veering left to join a driveway. Follow this to the B2110, reached midway between Upper Hartfield and Coleman's Hatch. (Grid ref: 460342)

Turn left, and a little over 100 yards later find a path on the right, immediately beyond the drive to Pond Cottage. This fence-enclosed path guides you to a meadow. Turn right, and on the far side go through a gateway and maintain direction to the far side of a second meadow, then bear half-left to the far corner of a third meadow. Here you go through a gateway with a large pond on the left (not shown on the OS map). Wander ahead beside a woodland shaw and come to Parrock Lane. (Grid ref: 457347) Cross directly ahead to a track. When this is joined by another veer right and follow it to the dismantled railway line, now adopted as the Forest Way Country Park, and Route B. (Grid ref: 457356) This alternative saves about $1/2$ mile.

Route B: Turn right and walk along the railway path for about $1^1/4$ miles, then take the second crossing path off to the right. (Grid ref: 475362) This is the route of the Main Walk as described below, leading directly to Hartfield.

Main Walk contd: Over the Forest Way the track/drive crosses the River Medway (4), here just a modest stream, and approaches the house known as Lower Parrock. Just beyond the Medway a wooden post directs a footpath to the right, over a ditch, then veering left to a junction of paths. Turn right through a meadow planted with trees, and through a gap on the far side. Cross an open field to a gate in a deer fence and continue ahead, passing a lake on the left (not marked on the OS map). Cross a stile in a boundary fence and on the far side of the next field go through a gate near the left-hand corner, then walk up the sloping meadow with views to Hartfield off to the right. At the top of the slope go through another field gate, and on the right a smaller gate in the deer fence leads into woodland. (Grid ref: 467364)

In a few paces come onto a narrow crossing path and bear right. Follow this through the wood descending to more meadows. The way continues ahead over a series of fields and meadows linked by stiles or gates, aiming towards Hartfield church. Coming to a footbridge over the Medway, cross once more the line of the old railway, where the route of **Route B** (Grid ref: 475362) joins us for the return to Hartfield. Maintain direction across the next field to a point about 20 yards left of a gateway where the path goes up a slope and enters a recreation ground. Through this come into the main street in Hartfield a short distance from the church.

Items of interest:

1: The Wealdway is met on several walks in this book. It's a long distance route of 82 miles which begins in Gravesend on the south bank of the Thames and ends at Beachy Head near Eastbourne. See *The Wealdway & The Vanguard Way* by Kev Reynolds (Cicerone Press).

2: Five Hundred Acre Wood is known to *Winnie the Pooh* fans as 'Hundred Acre Wood'. This is an extensive woodland of mixed species, including beech, oak and conifers, on the northern edge of Ashdown Forest, of which it was once part. It was enclosed for reafforestation in the late 17th century.

3: Pooh Corner is the name of the shop in Hartfield which specialises in Winnie the Pooh souvenirs. The building in which it is housed dates from about 1690.

4: The River Medway has several early tributaries here in East Sussex, one of which begins in a black bog on Ashdown Forest. As Kent's major river (it cuts right through the county to its estuary near Rochester) it has historically formed the divide between Men of Kent and Kentish Men, despite its birth in Sussex. Where we cross it is quite an insignificant stream, although a large part of the Kentish Medway is navigable - from Rochester upstream to Tonbridge. See *Medway Valley Walk* by Kev Reynolds (Kent County Council).

WALK 7
Ashurst Wood - Bassett's Manor - Ashurst Wood

Distance:	8¹/₂ miles
Map:	OS Explorer 135 (18) 'Ashdown Forest' 1:25,000
Start:	Ashurst Wood Post Office (Grid ref: 422368)
Access:	Via A22 midway between East Grinstead & Forest Row.
Parking:	With discretion in the village
Refreshments:	None on the route. Pub in Ashurst Wood.

Linking a series of meadows, fields and woodlands, footpaths adopted by this walk are mostly clearly defined and with finger posts or waymarks at

MAP 7

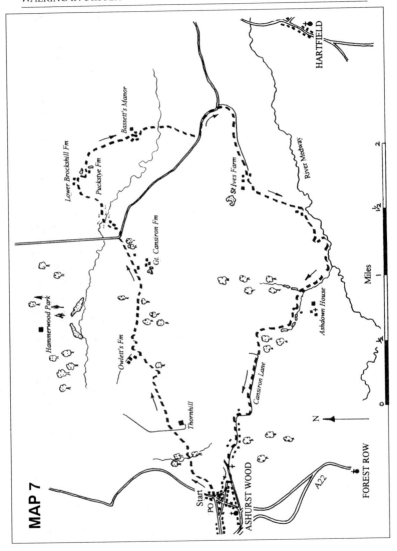

practically all strategic points. It is very much a rural walk, for there are neither villages nor hamlets along the way, and only on very rare occasions is the landscape fussed with more than a scattering of buildings - and these mostly farms or isolated houses. There is one marshy section to contend with, so good footwear is recommended, and since nettles threaten along the edge of the marsh, shorts cannot be advised. In springtime wild flowers brighten each woodland fringe (including bluebell, wild garlic, bugle and early purple orchid), and with such an abundance of trees it is evident that there's also plenty of birdlife. When we wandered these paths and bridleways we saw only two other walkers (and those near the end of the walk); the rest of the countryside seemed to be ours alone. Don't forget to take a packed lunch and a flask of drink with you as there are no refreshment facilities along the way.

*   *   *

Opposite the Post Office in Ashurst Wood the walk goes down a narrow concrete drive which begins between a house and a garage. After about 100 yards the drive curves left. At this point walk ahead on a footpath flanked by trees, and come to a crossing track known as Dirty Lane. Turn left and follow it to its end by a house. Continue directly ahead on a narrow path which soon descends into a strip of woodland. On the far side go up into a meadow with the large house, Thornhill, seen ahead to the right. Cross the meadow aiming for a point about 50 yards left of the right-hand boundary. Here a stile takes you onto Thornhill's driveway which is crossed into the meadow ahead. (Grid ref: 430375)

Walk across the meadow aiming slightly left ahead to another stile on a linking path behind a small brick building. This path leads into a large sloping meadow with views growing in extent. Follow the left-hand boundary through two meadows, descending into a broad but shallow valley with the buildings of Owlett's Farm ahead. Over another stile bear right along the edge of yet another meadow and go down to a farm drive where you bear left. Wander along this drive towards Owlett's Farm, but when it curves left, go over a stile on the right, then on a footbridge across a brook into a field. Turn left and follow the brook to a crossing track. Walk up the track a short distance. When it curves right, go into the field on the left, but within a few paces follow the dividing fence as it cuts back to the right. The way now leads alongside Holden Wood. Off to the left can be seen the large grey building of Hammerwood Park (1), set in a heavily wooded landscape. At the end of the wood cross a stile into the next field, which you cross following power lines. These lead through a woodland shaw and over another field to a crossing track. Bear left and walk along the track which soon becomes the drive for Great Cansiron Farm. This in turn leads to a narrow country road. (Grid ref: 453379)

Veer right along the road for about 130 yards, then go through a gateway on the left and descend a sloping grass path towards a house. Passing in front of the house keep to the left-hand fence boundary, cross the drive and continue down the slope over a second drive to pass between another house and its swimming pool. Maintain direction into a patch of woodland. A footbridge takes you over a stream, beyond which the way is guided across a marshy area by tall yellow-topped posts. Curving to the right through this marsh the actual path is a trifle vague in places, although its course is fairly obvious. A plank footbridge crosses the wettest area and at the far side you veer left through a corner of scrub to emerge into an open field. A footpath leads directly through this to a farm drive on the far side. (Grid ref: 459384)

Follow the drive to the right, soon passing Lower Brockshill Farm, beyond which you go up a slope with a pond on the left. Just after passing the tile-hung Puckstye Farm the drive ends at Puckstye House. Here you continue ahead on a grass footpath, go over a stile onto a slope of grassland dotted with trees and maintain direction into a more heavily wooded section. Out of this two gates take you into a large sloping meadow where you continue directly ahead along the lower boundary. Approaching farm buildings come onto a concrete farm drive. Curve right to walk through the farmyard of Bassett's Manor and continue along a driveway between meadows. After about a third of a mile this drive opens onto a narrow crossing road at Butcher's Cross. (Grid ref: 466370)

Turn left and walk along the road for 600 yards, at which point a drive leading to St Ives Farm cuts off to the right. This is also a bridleway. Follow the drive to the farm, ignoring various footpath options along the way - good views left over the valley cut by the infant River Medway, to Hartfield and Ashdown Forest. Passing through the farmyard come to a gate with a handsome half-timbered house ahead. Do not go through this gateway but cross a stile on the left into a field, and wander along its right-hand boundary, then through a gap into a second field where you go half-left and walk across the bottom far corner. Here you maintain direction through a narrow strip and into the next field where the path continues in the same direction. On the far side come to a junction of paths near a house. Walk ahead down a slope, then bear right over a small brook and go up onto a drive. Turn right, then left below another house to enter yet another field. (Grid ref: 456358)

Walk ahead along the left-hand boundary, then through a gap on the far side. Bear left round the edge of a very large sloping field, soon wandering alongside the River Medway, here a very minor stream. After a while a brook, mostly hidden among trees that form the field's western boundary, cuts down to join the Medway. The way follows this boundary to pass well to the right of Ashdown House. Where a few trees project into the field you continue ahead on a track to the left of a low barn with a rust-coloured corrugated iron roof. The track comes onto a drive and veers left. When the drive makes a sharp left-hand bend to approach Ashdown Farm, we go ahead slightly to the right and on alongside a woodland shaw. There's a pond partially hidden by the trees, and beyond this a second pond - this one open. Here the track forks. Veer right and walk up the slope alongside Highams Wood (2), soon passing a third pond not shown on the OS map.

Near the head of the slope the way curves left to pass through a stretch of woodland, then emerges at a junction of paths and bridleways on Cansiron Lane. (Grid ref: 439364) Walk ahead along this lane which, as it follows the crest of a ridge, enjoys long views to the right (as far as the Greensand Ridge in Kent), and left to Ashdown Forest. After almost $^1/_2$ mile the lane bends to the right, and for the next 200 yards is adopted by the Vanguard Way (2). The way curves left and passes a number of houses. Keep on Cansiron Lane until it ends by the entrance to Ashurst Wood Abbey. Now veer left and continue along a road, then break off to the right at School Lane. In a few paces this curves left, and just beyond the entrance to the local Primary School you veer right along Phoenix Lane which leads directly to Ashurst Wood Post Office where the walk began.

Items of interest:

1: Hammerwood Park, Great Cansiron Farm and Cansiron Lane are all names clearly associated with the Wealden iron industry which brought wealth to this part of Sussex. It is known that iron was worked in the Weald since Celtic times, and the early methods of smelting were adopted by both the Romans and Saxons. But in the 1500s hammers, weighing half a ton, were brought into use, and these were powered by water. Streams were dammed and 'hammer' ponds formed, and the furnaces were sometimes kept burning for thirty or forty weeks at a stretch. The amount of charcoal required to maintain constant heat had a profound effect on the woodland cover of the Weald. Today, echoes of the iron industry are carried in the names of houses, lanes and even villages, while the landscape retains many of the hammer ponds of old. Hammerwood Park itself was built in 1792 by Benjamin Latrobe. The house and grounds are open for guided tours on Saturdays, Wednesdays and Bank Holiday Mondays in summer.

2: Highams Wood is said to have supplied oaks for naval ship-building around the time of the Spanish Armada.

3: The Vanguard Way is a 62-mile long-distance recreational walking route which links East Croydon on the outskirts of London, with Seaford Head - with a recent extension to Newhaven. It's a fine walk that matches the Wealdway (Gravesend to Beachy Head) by crossing the North Downs, Greensand Ridge, the High Weald, Ashdown Forest and finally the South Downs. See *The Wealdway & The Vanguard Way* by Kev Reynolds (Cicerone Press).

WALK 8
Forest Row - St Ives Farm - Forest Row

Distance:	7 miles
Map:	OS Explorer 135 (18) 'Ashdown Forest' 1:25,000
Start:	The Foresters Arms, Forest Row (Grid ref: 426351)
Access:	Via A22, 4 miles south-east of East Grinstead; buses from East Grinstead, Tunbridge Wells and Uckfield
Parking:	Public car parks on B2110 (Hartfield road) near the start.
Refreshments:	None on walk. Pubs and cafés in Forest Row.

MAP 8

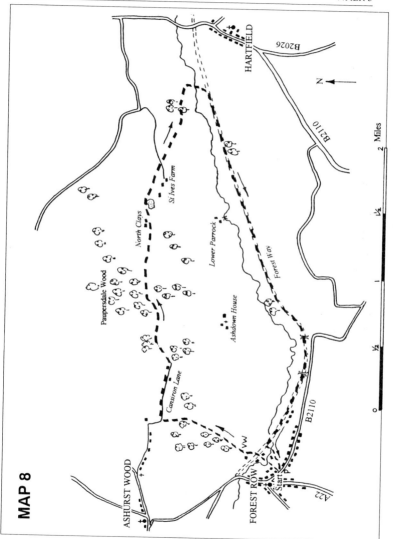

HARTFIELD

B2026

B2110

N

2 Miles
½
1
½
0

Paupersdale Wood

North Clays

Si Ives Farm

Lower Parrock

Forest Way

Cansron Lane

Ashdown House

ASHURST WOOD

FOREST ROW

B2110

A22

VW

Start

61

On the outward leg of this walk we follow the unmarked course of the Vanguard Way climbing steadily uphill to the narrow Cansiron Lane which traces a ridgetop with far-reaching views. The lane leads to fields, meadows and woodland on the way to St Ives Farm before sloping gently down to the low valley of the infant Medway. Return to Forest Row is along the Forest Way, on the bed of a dismantled railway. This is a pleasant walk through an uncluttered countryside.

*   *   *

The Foresters Arms is beside the B2110 on the corner of Station Road, about 200 yards south of the Parish Church. To begin the walk go along Station Road to its end by some factory buildings. Bear slightly left, then right on a footpath which crosses a narrow lane/track. The path, adopted by the Vanguard Way (1) goes along the right-hand side of a pumping station and soon begins to rise alongside a woodland shaw. After a while cross a stile into the shaw and continue uphill. Near the head of the slope the way becomes something of a sunken trail leading to Cansiron Lane at a sharp bend. (Grid ref: 432365)

Bear right, now leaving the Vanguard Way, and follow the lane to its end. A track cuts off to the left, while there are three other footpath/bridleway options. Take that which crosses a stile half-left ahead. Walk across the field to the far corner, aiming towards the right-hand end of a woodland outlined with ash trees. There you cross another stile into the adjacent field, follow the edge of the woodland for about 20 yards and continue ahead once the wood cuts back to the left. A big panoramic view is enjoyed as you wander across this field, which is partially surrounded by woods. On the far side cross a stile in a field bay and enter Paupersdale Wood. (Grid ref: 446366)

In a few paces come to a firebreak, or ride, and bear left (the OS map is faulty in regard to this wood). The 'firebreak' soon leads to the edge of the wood and a crossing track. Continue ahead along the left-hand edge of a large hilltop field, and maintain direction alongside a second field, on the far side of which you go through a gap and along the edge of a third large field. The spire of Hartfield Church may be seen ahead, $1^{3}/_{4}$ miles away, with Ashdown Forest rising to the right. Halfway along this field pass a farm on your left (North Clays), where there's a crossing path. If you were to take the right-hand path it would save about 1¹/₂ miles - it descends to Lower Parrock and the Forest Way, which leads back to Forest Row. We, however, continue ahead and at the far boundary cross a stile near a pond, with a campsite nearby. (Grid ref: 458367)

Pass along the left-hand side of the pond and cut through the open field ahead. On the far side go through a gap in the hedge onto a narrow lane (this leads to St Ives Farm) which you cross to a stile in a deer fence. Bear half-left and walk across to a field gate about 100 yards down the slope. Through the gate maintain direction to the far right-hand end of a woodland shaw. Once again there are fine views to Ashdown Forest. In the corner of the field there's another gate, but to the left of this you cross a stile in the deer fence and enter woodland, which is full of bluebells in springtime. The path slopes gently downhill, and on emerging from the trees crosses a narrow meadow to a gate. Through this maintain direction along the left-hand edge of the next field. On coming to a third field walk through it to the far side, then instead of crossing a stile ahead, bear right and walk down the left-hand edge on a bridleway to reach a sturdy wooden bridge over the Medway. (Grid ref: 473360)

Over the bridge turn right, go through a low railway arch and turn sharp left up a few steps onto the former railway track, the Forest Way (2). Bear left and follow this straight and even path for three miles back to Forest Row (3).

The walk takes you between fields, and on the outskirts of Forest Row passes beneath two bridges, goes along the back of houses and eventually crosses the Medway stream. About 100 yards beyond the stream come to the edge of an industrial estate and turn left on a footpath among trees. The path soon leads alongside the boundary fence of a timber yard. When the fence cuts back to the right, bear right and come to an open grass area near The Foresters Arms where the walk began.

Items of interest:

1: The Vanguard Way is a recreational long distance walk devised in 1980 by the Croydon-based Vanguards Rambling Club. It begins by East Croydon railway station, and originally finished 62 miles later on Seaford Head. It has recently been extended to Newhaven. See *The Wealdway & The Vanguard Way* by Kev Reynolds (Cicerone Press).

2: The Forest Way is a linear country park established on the line of the defunct railway which once ran between East Grinstead and Groombridge by way of Forest Row. For much of its 9$^{1}/_{2}$ mile length it follows the course of the infant River Medway. Bought by East Sussex County Council in 1971, the country park was opened three years later.

3: Forest Row grew from a group of lodges used to accommodate Royal hunting parties on Ashdown Forest, and became a stage on the London to Eastbourne coaching route.

WALK 9
Forest Row - Weir Wood Reservoir - Forest Row

Distance:	8 miles
Maps:	OS Explorer 135 (18) 'Ashdown Forest' 1:25,000
Start:	Forest Row Parish Church (Grid ref: 424352)
Access:	Via A22, 4 miles south-east of East Grinstead.
Parking:	Public car parks on B2110 (Hartfield road) 200 yards from start.
Refreshments:	None on the walk, but pubs and cafés in Forest Row.

On this walk we make a partial circuit of Weir Wood Reservoir - but never quite along its shoreline. Sometimes we are close to it, with birdlife as well as sailing activity providing entertainment. At other times we gaze down on it from a lovely green hilltop; then the reservoir takes on the appearance of a natural lake contained within the gentle embrace of wooded hills. But although the reservoir forms the dominant feature of the walk, it is not the only one, for there are long meadow and woodland sections, innocent streams and the grey studded ruin of Brambletye House that punctuates the landscape with its own essential character. If you have binoculars it would be worth taking them with you, especially for use in a hide built alongside the reservoir for birdwatchers.

*   *   *

Holy Trinity Church stands at the junction of A22 and B2110. To begin the walk head away from the church in the direction of East

Kneppmill Pond near Knepp Castle *(Walk 18)*
Ypres Tower, built in the 13th century and now a museum *(Walk 19)*

Barcombe Mill Pond *(Walk 26)*
The River Arun, near Houghton Bridge *(Walk 30)*

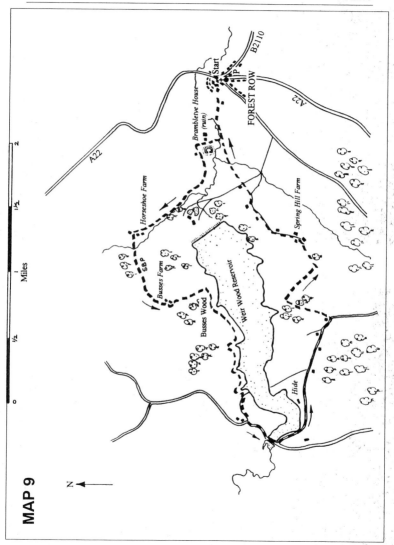

MAP 9

N ←

Miles
0   ½   1   1½   2

Start
P
FOREST ROW
B2110
A22
A22
Brambletye House (ruin)
Horseshoe Farm
SBP
Busses Farm
Busses Wood
Weir Wood Reservoir
Spring Hill Farm
Hide

Grinstead, then take the first turning on the left (Riverside) beside Brambletye Hotel. Turn left again behind the hotel and walk ahead to Kennard Court, a development of private houses, where a footpath breaks off to the right. This leads beyond the houses into a rough, sloping meadow where it then forks. Ignore the left-hand option and go up the slope to a stile in an archway of holly trees. Over this enter a hilltop meadow and continue ahead to the lower right-hand corner where you go through a kissing gate, over a track and alongside a barn. Beyond the barn cross a stile on the left by Burnthouse Farm, and walk down a grass track with the ruins of Brambletye House seen a short distance away. The track leads into a field and a footpath continues slightly left ahead to another stile on the far side. Over this walk alongside a tributary of the River Medway through a meadow planted with young trees, and come to a crossing bridleway. (Grid ref: 416352)

   Turn right, then passing Brambletye Manor Farm with the grey turreted ruins behind it, reach a crossing track/driveway. Bear left to pass between the garden boundary of a converted barn, and a partially concealed moat. When the track/driveway curves right to the house, veer left along a continuing track between fields. Remain on the track as it bends to the right. At a junction of paths maintain direction ahead and walk through a narrow woodland shaw above a stream. Out of the trees the way continues through a patch of scrub, then across a field. On the far side cross a stile into a second field and make for the far right-hand corner where a fenced path leads alongside Horseshoe Farm and onto a drive. Pass another house, and about 50 yards later turn left on the West Sussex Border Path (1). (Grid ref: 406362)

   The path crosses a stream by footbridge, immediately beyond which a second footbridge heads to the right, but we ignore this and instead go through a field gate and walk ahead along the right-hand edge of two fields, mostly alongside woodland. At the end of the second field enter a meadow across which Busses Farm is seen. The path leads towards the right-hand side of the farm - a narrow, pink, tile-hung house. Go through a gate onto a concrete drive where East Grinstead may be seen off to the right. Approach the farmhouse, then go right then left to pass round barns before coming onto a tree-lined track that slopes down towards Weir Wood Reservoir (2).

(Grid ref: 397356) The reservoir is set in a shallow valley flanked by gently rising fields and meadows with wood-crowned hills above.

Halfway down the slope a bridleway cuts off through a meadow, but we continue down the line of trees still following the West Sussex Border Path. At the foot of the slope bear right through Busses Wood. Continue along the north side of the reservoir following a clearly defined path guided by a chain-link fence that sadly denies public access to the shoreline. A series of meadows and little wooded areas are linked by stiles, passing below Stone Hill - a rise studded with limestone outcrops - and coming to a narrow lane by a gate. (Grid ref: 386348)

Turn right and walk up this lane to its junction with a crossing road, then bear left and wander down the road to the western end of the reservoir. Just beyond this take the first turning left and follow Legsheath Lane for 1¹/₄ miles, soon passing a birdwatchers' hide. After passing two minor roads cutting left, the lane makes a sharp right-hand bend at the top of a hill by a house. Leave the lane here, cross a stile on the left and walk down a sloping field to its bottom far corner with fine views over the reservoir to East Grinstead in the distance. Go through a kissing gate into a wood named Alder Moors. At first the path through is a little marshy, but it soon improves, and as you emerge onto a track turn sharply right and go through a gate into a meadow. (Grid ref: 397344)

Walk through this to its highest part and locate a field gate leading into another sloping meadow, which you cross to its far right-hand corner. A short distance from the corner there's a field gate and a stile. Do not cross, but instead walk on round the edge of the meadow, turning left with it and starting down the slope to another stile in the hedge on the right. Over this walk across to yet another stile seen on the far side, from which a wide vista is gained - down to the reservoir on the left, and far ahead to a blue line of hills and folding ridges in between. Descend the slope towards Mudbrooks House, then bear left along a track which becomes a driveway passing Spring Hill Farm. (Grid ref: 405343)

Remain on the driveway. It swings right by South Park Farm, and about 150 yards later comes to the edge of a wood. Bear left here and take a footpath through the wood. On coming to a narrow crossing lane by a house, cross directly ahead and maintain direction over a field with the grey ruin of Brambletye House once more in view. A kissing gate gives access to a meadow with a plantation of trees, and over this you come to a crossing bridleway. (Grid ref: 416352) Directly ahead is the footpath which leads to Burnthouse Farm used on the outward route. Follow the now familiar path back to Forest Row.

Items of interest:

1: The West Sussex Border Path strikes south from East Grinstead and more or less traces the borders of East and West Sussex for 38 miles as a spur off the main Sussex Border Path.

2: Weir Wood Reservoir covers an area of about 280 acres, and was formed when the Upper Medway Valley was dammed in 1950. Part of the reservoir is now a nature reserve. It is stocked with trout and access to the shore is restricted to anglers.

WALK 10
King's Standing - Heron's Ghyll - King's Standing

Distance:	7 miles
Map:	OS Explorer 135 (18) 'Ashdown Forest' 1:25,000
Start:	King's Standing Car Park (Grid ref: 474302)
Access:	By road, 4½ miles south of Hartfield, at B2026/B2188 junction.
Parking:	King's Standing Car Park Ashdown Forest
Refreshments:	Pub at Poundgate

Midway between the North and the South Downs, the heights of Ashdown Forest provide expansive views, among the best of which are seen on this circular walk. There is a sense of remoteness about this countryside, the more surprising for the fact that Crowborough lies but a short distance to the east. But Crowborough is hidden beyond a wooded ridge - as other surrounding communities are also hidden - and even on a bright Bank Holiday you can enjoy the bracken- and birch-crowded paths with only birdsong for company. There are a few modest hills to contend with, several areas of mixed woodland, and the great open heath that blazes purple in summer.

*   *   *

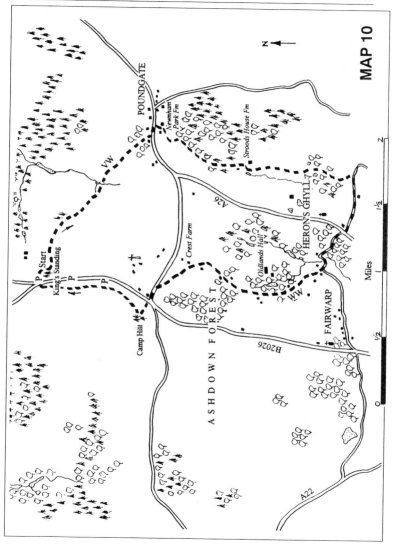

MAP 10

69

From the car park at the B2026/B2188 junction, go to the nearby group of pine trees known as King's Standing Clump, pass round its left-hand side, then turn right at a junction of paths to keep alongside the trees. This path is shared by the Vanguard Way (1), although there is no sign to indicate the fact. Just beyond the clump bear left to wander along one of the highest parts of Ashdown Forest with views now across a valley to a wooded ridge. To the right a tall mast can be seen. This marks the site of a former radio station that broadcast propaganda messages during the war. As you progress so views grow in extent, with the South Downs forming a distant horizon. Beyond a minor clump of pine trees the path, a bridleway, goes down a slope a short distance, then veers right while a narrow path continues ahead. Remain on the bridleway and ease steadily downhill. At the foot of the slope a footbridge takes you over a minor stream - one of the sources of the Medway, Kent's major river. Up the slope beyond ignore alternative paths and continue on the main bridleway which leads through a lightly wooded section before coming to the A26 by the side of Old Bell House. (Grid ref: 491289)

Turn left and shortly before reaching The Crow and Gate pub cross the road to a stile in the hedge behind a telephone kiosk. Follow the left-hand boundary of a field, go through a gate to the right of a dutch barn and walk ahead along a drive between houses at Newnham Park Farm. Enter the field ahead by a gate and bear right, then cross a stile in the corner into the next field. Walk down the right-hand side, with long views to the South Downs. Halfway along the field cross left to a woodland corner where the continuing path takes you along the inner right-hand edge of Newnham Park Wood. Eventually the path leads out to a field where you keep the wood on your left. At the bottom corner of the field re-enter the woods, following a deer fence to a cottage. Out of the woods the way continues now towards Stroods House Farm, but shortly before reaching its drive a signpost sends you among trees on the right, down a slope towards a pond. Above this come onto the drive and bear left for a few paces, then cut right following a line of posts across a long meadow below Stroods House Farm, a large white imposing building with fine views east. (Grid ref: 488277)

On coming to a line of trees the Vanguard Way breaks away left up some steps, but our path remains in the meadow and follows the trees to the right. In the bottom corner enter Quarry Wood and continue ahead when an alternative track breaks off to the right. Rise above a small pond, and reaching the end of the wood the way veers left to a narrow lane. Bear right and follow the lane as far as the A26, soon passing off to the left a curious navigational aid which looks as though it has been abandoned by a UFO! Reach the A26 by Heron's Ghyll Lodge (Grid ref: 479266), bear right and a few paces later go left along Oldlands Hill. Twisting downhill through woods pass Oldlands Farm, soon after which the road is crossed by a stream - there is a footbridge. Up the slope come to a set of wrought-iron gates at the entrance to Oldlands Hall (2) opposite the white weatherboarded Oldlands Corner Cottage. (Grid ref: 475268)

Turn half-right and walk up a driveway between the gates and the cottage, now on the route of the Wealdway (3). Soon join a bridleway parallel to the drive on its right-hand side, and come once more within the boundaries of Ashdown Forest. After a while the bridleway crosses the drive, veers right to join a broad open ride, and passes Payne's Hill Cottages. Rising gently up a slope flanked by bracken and birch, keep alert for a WW oak marker post which directs a narrow footpath slightly right ahead. This crosses a drive, then descends a slope to a second drive where you bear left. When it ends by Brown's Brook Cottage, continue ahead where a footbridge over a narrow stream takes a path into woodland. (Grid ref: 473278)

The way twists up the woodland slope to the end of another drive. Walk ahead round a holly hedge by a cottage, then continue to rise among bracken and gorse. On coming to another crossing drive walk ahead, but shortly after rejoin it until it curves to the right. Now bear left for a few paces, then go half right to a stile. The path cuts alongside the garden boundary of Little Barnden and brings you to yet another stony drive. Wander up this, and you'll soon be rewarded with big views behind you. After passing a cottage the drive swings right. At this point leave it in favour of a footpath on the left which leads to a minor road. Bear left to the B2026. (Grid ref: 471288)

Cross directly ahead through a gate and walk towards the pine clump on Camp Hill. Immediately before reaching this leave the Wealdway at last to follow a broad ride on the right. This runs

View across Ashdown Forest to Old Lodge, from Camp Hill

parallel with the road, and grants open views across a vast sweep of heather. At a broad crossing path continue ahead, the way rising slightly and coming to another crossing path with a bench seat on the right. Maintain direction, still rising. The ride forks and you take the right branch ahead. At the head of the slope note King's Standing Clump off to the right. When a path cuts to the right, wander to the road and bear left for a few paces to reach the car park where the walk began.

Items of interest:

1: The Vanguard Way is a long-distance recreational route which leads from East Croydon Station to Seaford Head, with a recent extension to Newhaven. See *The Wealdway & The Vanguard Way* by Kev Reynolds (Cicerone Press).

2: Oldlands Hall owes its ancestry to the iron industry, for the estate was actively involved in the business of casting iron. The Romans were also smelting here, and remains of a Roman building, together with pieces of pottery dating from the first century AD, have been unearthed. So too have the skeletal remains of several bodies.

3: The Wealdway is met several times within these pages. This 82 mile long distance walk begins at Gravesend on the Kent bank of the Thames, and continues as far as Beachy Head, in so doing it explores the landscape highlights of two counties. See *The Wealdway & The Vanguard Way* - see Item 1 above.

WALK 11
Duddleswell - Nutley - Camp Hill - Duddleswell

Distance:	6³/₄ miles
Map:	OS Explorer 135 (18) 'Ashdown Forest' 1:25,000
Start:	Duddleswell Car Park (Grid ref: 467279)
Access:	By road Duddleswell is located 2¹/₂ miles north of Maresfield on B2026. The car park is situated opposite Duddleswell Tearooms.
Parking:	Duddleswell. Several other car parks on Ashdown Forest - see map.
Refreshments:	Duddleswell Tearooms.

Ashdown Forest offers exhilarating walks with extensive views that stretch to both the North and the South Downs, as well as overlooking a large area of the High Weald. There are numerous footpaths, tracks and bridleways, not all of which are marked on the OS maps, and very few waymarks or signposts have been erected to help walkers find their way. This great region of heath and woodland is, then, a splendid place to get lost in! The circuit described here should, hopefully, help you explore some of the best the Forest has to offer, without getting lost. It meanders among regions of bracken and gorse, crosses open spaces bright with heather on broad rides, and winds through woodlands cut by rust-coloured streams that betray the presence of iron-ore, whose extraction brought wealth to the iron-masters who built their large houses on the Forest rim. The walk visits a small village, the oldest working windmill in Sussex, and a viewpoint marked by a post to celebrate the opening of The Wealdway long-distance path which crosses the Forest on its way from the Thames to the sea.

*   *   *

Leave the car park opposite Duddleswell Tearooms on a footpath which strikes away from the left-hand (southern) end through a metal squeeze stile. At first among bracken, the footpath comes to a broad ride. Go up the slope a few paces, then find the continuing path on the right which soon slopes downhill. Joining a crossing path veer left. On reaching the drive of Little Gassons, follow this for a few paces, and when it curves left continue ahead to another drive and maintain direction. The way leads between two more houses, with views now reaching to the South Downs. The drive curves

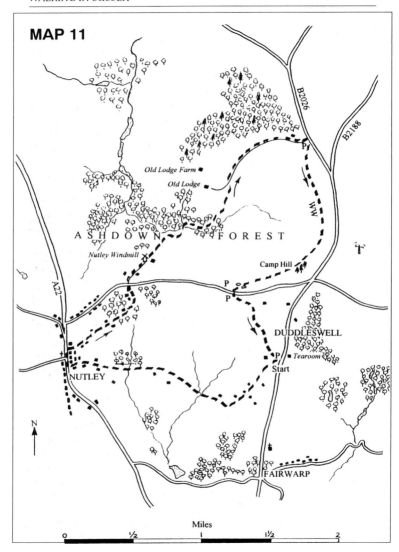

right towards another house, and just as this comes in sight, bear left on a footpath. Cross a track (a barn seen to the left), and a few yards later turn right on a broad bare-earth path. Nutley now appears on the ridge ahead. When the path forks continue ahead and descend to the foot of a slope where two small streams come together. (Grid ref: 458274)

On crossing the second footbridge walk up the slope ahead on another broad ride. On the brow of the hill continue ahead over a crossing track, then slope down into a ghyll and another stream. Soon after starting up the next slope cut left on a footpath. Cross a track leading to Lower Misbourne Farm, and after going through some trees you'll come to the boundary fence of Upper Misbourne Farm. Bear right, pass through a gate near the farm entrance and continue ahead, over a crossing path to join a broader path heading towards Nutley. This becomes a wide fire-break, descends to another stream by a small wood, then forks. Stay with the main path rising uphill. This curves right near the top of the slope. Ignore alternative paths and you'll eventually come to a drive leading between houses, then onto the main road (A22) at Nutley. (Grid ref: 443278)

Turn right, and soon after passing the church of St James the Less (on the left) turn right into School Lane. Follow this for half a mile until it curves to enter the grounds of a house named Morrisfield, where a footpath goes through a gate and into woods. Come to a drive near a pink-walled house and continue ahead. Rejoining the drive soon after follow this until, about 30 yards beyond the second of two houses (Alma Cottage), you must bear left at a crossing path. This brings you to a country road opposite a drive leading to Nutley Windmill. (Grid ref: 449288)

Cross with care and follow the drive to the windmill (1). Immediately past the mill, go through a metal squeeze stile and on a footpath descend a slope among trees. Cross a broad ride and continue downhill. Go over a second ride, but at a T-junction of paths, turn right. On emerging to the open edge of the Forest, veer left on another ride, then break away a few paces later on the second path on the left which leads into woodland. At path junctions keep ahead to gain a footbridge over a stream. The way now climbs a slope, at first among trees, then contouring to the right to a fork. A waymark on a tree directs the path left, then over a stile by some pine trees into the grounds of Old Lodge Estate. Follow the right-hand boundary of a park-like meadow, then over two stiles into the next pasture on the right with lovely views across the vast heathland of Ashdown Forest (2). Go up the left-hand edge of the meadow, over another stile by a field gate and into a third pasture. At the top left-hand corner go out to a driveway. Follow this all the way to the B2026. (Grid ref: 470305)

Immediately to the right, walk through a small car park, and along a footpath used by the Wealdway (3). Go through a gate to a junction of rides. Ignore that which branches right and continue ahead to cross an open stretch of Forest with magnificent views. Keep on this main ride as far as Camp Hill, a stand of Scots pine at a junction of tracks where there are several bench seats from which to enjoy a splendid panorama, which includes the imposing Old Lodge to the north-west. At this point the Wealdway breaks off to the left, but we maintain direction on a continuing broad ride which eventually slopes down to Ellison's Pond by a car park. Veer left to a road and cross into another car park (The Hollies). (Grid ref: 462286)

At the entrance bear left on a broad sandy path flanked by gorse bushes rising up a slope. Ignore alternative paths and keep to the main one which soon curves to the right to include Chanctonbury Ring on the distant South Downs in its view. The way goes down a slope and forks. Keep directly ahead towards a house, and on coming to its drive turn left to return to the Duddleswell car park where the walk began.

Items of interest:

1: Nutley Windmill is claimed to be the oldest working windmill in Sussex. This trestle post mill was built about 1700, and has been restored by members of the Uckfield and District Preservation Society, who open it to the public on the last Sunday of each month from Easter to September - 2.30-5.30pm.

2: Ashdown Forest was called "the most villainously ugly spot I ever saw in England" by William Cobbett who crossed it in 1822. But to the thousands of visitors who flock here on bright weekends throughout the year, it is an invigorating place with some of the loveliest panoramic views south of London. The Forest consists today of 6,400 acres of open heath and woodland managed by a board of Conservators made up of local Council Members and elected Commoners. The Romans pushed their road from London to Lewes across the highest part, and small stretches of paving can still be seen today. By Norman times Commoners' Rights were well established, but during the Middle Ages most of the Forest had been claimed as a hunting ground and divided among the more powerful landowners, leaving the Commoners to fight for the right to continue to graze their animals and collect firewood. In 1987 the last private owners of Ashdown Forest, the De La Warr family, sold it to East Sussex County Council, and the public now enjoys the right of access on foot over the whole Forest. (For a fascinating account of the Forest's history, see Garth Christian's *Ashdown Forest*, published by the Society of Friends of Ashdown Forest, 1967.)

3: The Wealdway crosses Ashdown Forest from north to south on its 82-mile journey from Gravesend in Kent to Beachy Head. It was opened by the chairman of the Countryside Commission on 27 September 1981 at Camp Hill. (See *The Wealdway & The Vanguard Way* by Kev Reynolds, Cicerone Press.)

WALK 12
West Hoathly - Crawley Down - West Hoathly

Distance:	8 miles
Map:	OS Explorer 135 (18) 'Ashdown Forest' 1:25,000
Start:	Finche Field, West Hoathly (Grid ref: 366326)
Access:	Via minor road leading into the village from Sharpthorne, about 5 miles south-west of Forest Row.
Parking:	Finche Field
Refreshments:	None en route, but pub and shop in West Hoathly.

This is a walk of ponds, lakes and woodland; a circular tour of High Weald country west of Weir Wood Reservoir, and with the Bluebell Railway marking its eastern limit. Other than sneaking to the outskirts of Crawley Down, it visits no villages, and passes but few farms. This is countryside inhabited by songbirds, fish and grazing cows, while the paths that meander through are typical of the ancient routes of passage used by

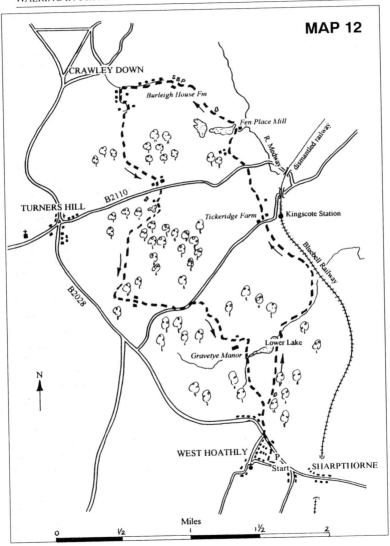

MAP 12

countless generations of country folk going about their daily tasks, long before the Mechanical Age brought about a greatly reduced workforce on the land. Now only an occasional tractor trundles across the fields, from whose paths long views show the distant acres that made this such a productive county. Wandering the green miles it is only the circling aircraft of Gatwick that disturb the songs of birds and the lazy splash of a fish coming up for a fly.

*   *   *

Finche Field is located at the eastern end of West Hoathly (1), between the junction of roads near Sharpthorne. There's a car park and picnic area, 'given for the enjoyment of the public in 1965'. From here walk along the tarmac footpath towards West Hoathly village, passing the picnic area with its fine views, and on coming to houses bear right on a path that crosses two fields and descends to a road. Turn left and walk along the road for about 200 yards as far as a junction. At this point cut off to the right alongside a garage, beyond which a narrow surfaced drive leads to a footpath on the edge of Shagswell Wood. At a junction of paths continue ahead (the left-hand option is used on the return). In a few paces the path forks. Take the upper branch ahead, and then cross a stile on the left above a small pond to enter a field. (Grid ref: 365333)

Follow the right-hand boundary for about 150 yards, then cut directly down the slope to a footpath signpost seen in a gap in the trees ahead. Continue through the gap into another field, and maintain direction to its far left-hand corner where the continuing path enters a projection of Hastings Wood. To the left lies Gravetye Lower Lake, owned by the Forestry Commission. (A path round the lake is open daily, except in winter, from 10.00am-dusk. Private fishing; no picnics.) Emerging from the wood, with Home Farm seen ahead, turn right and walk round the edge of two fields. At the end of the second of these go through another section of woodland, and out of this go ahead along the edge of the next field. Three-quarters of the way round this cross a stile on the right onto a narrow surfaced drive. Bear left, and passing through a gateway come onto a narrow lane. (Grid ref: 371348)

With the Bluebell Railway (2) off to the right walk along the lane for a little over half a mile until you come to a T junction. Cross with care and enter the farmyard of Tickeridge Farm. Passing between the farmhouse and a barn the drive curves to the right, at which point there are two field gates ahead. Go through the right-hand of these and down a slope to a footbridge seen on the far side of a field. Over the bridge the continuing path is guided by a fence alongside a woodland shaw, then curves right to pass through the shaw above a small pond. Keep along the right-hand side of two more fields to the B2110. (Grid ref: 364363)

Turn left for a short distance, and when the road curves you walk down a drive on the right. This leads to Millwood and Fen Place Mill. The Mill is a lovely building set in splendid grounds, and with a large millpond on the left - one of the sources of the River Medway. Pass to the left of the house, beyond which there's a junction of paths. Take the left-hand option, and about 30 yards later cross a stile on the right and wander round the edge of successive fields on a broad grass path guided by a fence. After passing above a pond continue as far as a woodland corner where a stile leads into a large field. Bear left and cross to a field gate on the far side, there to join the route of the West Sussex Border Path. (Grid ref: 357373)

Follow this heading left, soon passing Burleigh House Farm on a track which leads to the farm drive. This becomes a narrow lane (Burleigh Lane), along which you wander for about a third of a mile, passing several houses on the way. On coming to the junction with Sandhill Lane turn left and follow this lane to its end. At the gateway of Sandhill Farm bear half right on a broad path which becomes a very pleasant tree-lined trail flanked by foxgloves and masses of cranesbill in early summer. The way descends to a stream crossed by footbridge, then through a patch of woodland. At the head of the slope come to a driveway by a house. Follow the drive as far as the B2110 which is reached by the entrance to Alexander House. (Grid ref: 354360)

Bear left for a few paces, then cross the road to another drive/ track sloping down into a lovely wooded valley. Down the slope the drive curves right, with a footpath continuing ahead. This leads to another stream crossing, over which you bear right. Passing yet another pond on the right come into a sloping meadow and walk up this to the left. Near the head of the meadow continue among trees, then maintain direction along the left-hand edge of another meadow. As you enter a second meadow through a gap cross a stile on the left and go ahead among trees with a boundary fence on your right. Halfway up the slope cross another stile, continue ahead, and soon go along the left-hand edge of a woodland. Beyond this maintain direction on the edge of a field before being guided into a tree-shrouded gully that leads into a long woodland shaw. The shaw eventually brings you to a crossing path on the edge of Selsfield Common. (Grid ref: 348346)

Turn left, go up a few timber-braced steps to a second path junction. Again take the left-hand option and wander ahead among birch and oak trees, bracken and bilberries, and about 200 yards later reach a kissing gate. Through this a broad grass path between fences leads to a drive serving Selsfield Place. Continue ahead to a gate with a large white house on the left. Through the gate go ahead along a farm track that rewards with a big Wealden panorama, and eventually come to country road (Vowels Lane). Bear left, but when the road makes a sharp left-hand bend, enter the driveway of a house called Moatlands, on the right. Almost immediately cut off to the left on a footpath among trees and rhododendrons, and with a carpet of bluebells in spring. The path curves right and goes alongside a wall, then slopes downhill, in woodland, to a crossing track. (Grid ref: 360341)

Bear left and before long you're wandering just above the grey building of Gravetye Manor (3), an hotel with splendid gardens bright with rhododendrons and azaleas spilling down the hillside. On reaching the driveway by the main gate, continue ahead onto a broad grass path that swings right and descends into a tight knuckle valley, near the foot of which the path forks. The left branch goes alongside Gravetye Lower Lake (met earlier on the walk at its north-eastern end), while the right-hand option is the one to take back to West Hoathly. This brings you out of the trees at the foot of a sloping field. Here you turn right and wander along the lower boundary, and at the far corner maintain direction on the edge of another woodland. The path is soon joined by another coming from the right. Leave the woods by a few stone steps and continue up the right-hand edge of another sloping field. Towards the top of the field the path goes through a small gap into the adjacent field. Continue up the slope and at its highest point enter Shagswell Wood. Over the stile bear right and rejoin the outward route. Follow the path to the garage at the junction of roads on the outskirts of West Hoathly, and return to the car park where the walk began.

Items of interest:

1: West Hoathly is an attractive hilltop village dating from Saxon times, and with smuggling connections. The church of St Margaret is more than 900 years old, and tradition has it that smugglers used to signal from the tower to announce a meeting in the Cat Inn. Nearby, the timber-framed, 15th century Priest House is now a museum in the care of the Sussex Archaeological Society (open daily March to October), while the 17th century Manor House is said to have formed part of the divorce settlement made by Henry VIII for Anne of Cleves.

2: The Bluebell Railway is a romantic steam service restored and operated largely by a team of enthusiastic volunteers; the first standard gauge preserved line in Britain. The railway operates a 10-mile service between Sheffield Park Station and Kingscote Station (the latter passed on the walk), via Horsted Keynes, and there's a special vintage bus service linking Kingscote with the mainline rail network at East Grinstead.

3: Gravetye Manor was built for iron-master Richard Infield in 1598, but its noted gardens were created by William Robertson, author of *The English Flower Garden*, between 1880 and 1935. It is now owned by the Forestry Commission, as is much of the surrounding woodland and the Lower Lake. The manor house has been converted into an hotel, but there's public access (parties of not more than four people) to certain rooms on Fridays only, by prior arrangement, while the grounds are open on Tuesdays and Fridays, from 10.00am-5.00pm by a marked path.

WALK 13
Horsted Keynes - Twyford Farm - Horsted Keynes

Distance:	6 miles (or 8 miles by route A option)
Map:	OS Explorer 135 (18) 'Ashdown Forest' 1:25,000
Start:	Horsted Keynes Post Office (Grid ref: 384283) or (route

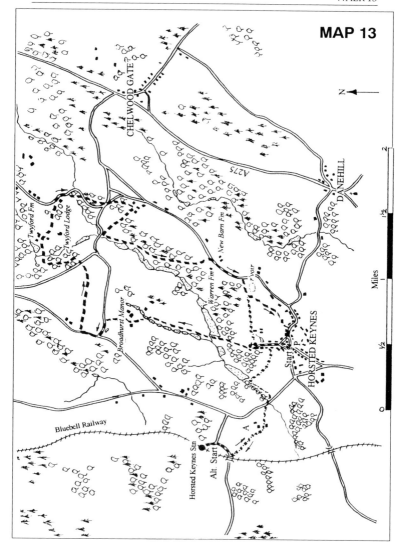

MAP 13

N ◀—

Miles

CHELWOOD GATE

DANEHILL

A275

Twyford Fm

Twyford Lodge

New Barn Fm

Warren Fm

River

Broadhurst Manor

Start

P

HORSTED KEYNES

A

Bluebell Railway

Horsted Keynes Stn

Alt. Start

2

1½

1

½

0

	A) Horsted Keynes Railway Station - Bluebell Line (Grid ref: 372293)
Access:	By bus from East Grinstead or Haywards Heath. By train on the Bluebell Railway (Sheffield Park - Kingscote/East Grinstead) - for walkers following route A option. By road, take minor road west from Danehill on A275.
Parking:	Free car park by Horsted Keynes playing field off Chapel Lane near Post Office. (Grid ref: 384283)
Refreshments:	Pubs and shops in Horsted Keynes. None on route.

The trim village of Horsted Keynes lies in secluded country untouched by busy roads. High Wealden hills roll among woodland and meadow, while numerous lakes and ponds fill the intervening valleys. This circular walk follows a series of tracks, footpaths and bridleways north of the village, sometimes beside those lakes and ponds, often through woodland, but with lovely hinted views to surprise and delight between the trees. At all times of the year this makes a very fine outing, although sections of bridleway can be muddy after a period of prolonged rain. Walkers who come by the Bluebell Railway should follow directions for route A, while those who reach Horsted Keynes by bus or private vehicle should follow Main Walk directions.

*   *   *

Route A: On leaving Horsted Keynes Station turn right along the approach road, then bear right at a junction. Immediately before reaching a railway bridge cross a stile on the left into a large meadow. The path aims across this in the direction of the left-hand end of a line of trees, where you join a track. Go through a gate and bear right. Cross to farm buildings and another gate, then bear left by a small barn. A few yards later turn right towards the farmhouse. The way then takes you along the left-hand side of the house and down a hedge-lined track. Soon leave it through a gate on the left, then cross half-right through a sloping meadow to gain a country road by a stile next to a field gate. (Grid ref: 377285)

Bear right along the road, cross a stream and immediately turn left by a large black barn. A track then leads to the southern end of a lake where you turn sharp right on a footpath among trees. Out of the trees the fence-enclosed path leads between meadows on the approach to Horsted Keynes (1). Come onto Church Lane by some cottages and turn left to St Giles' Church to join the Main Walk. (Grid ref: 384286)

Main Walk: From the Post Office/shop at the western end of the village green, cross the main road and go down a narrow tarmac lane beside The Forge. This leads to Church Lane which you follow as far as the slender-spired church of St Giles (Grid ref: 384286). Stay on the lane as it skirts the left-hand side of the churchyard. Ignoring a path which cuts left, continue ahead on a track leading into woods. This slopes downhill to the bottom end of a lake, and beyond this passes alongside a string of smaller lakes, or ponds. Eventually the track forks near a small barn. Take the left-hand option. This makes a sharp right-hand bend by a half-timbered house, then passes the entrance gates to Broadhurst Manor. Bear left along the drive to reach Hurstwood Lane. (Grid ref: 386304)

Turn left, and on reaching a T-junction bear right. About 200yds later cross a stile on the right and walk ahead along the top edge of three meadows linked by stiles. On entering a fourth, the path maintains direction on a grass divider between fields, on the far side of which you come to another narrow lane. Cross directly ahead into Grinstead Wood. The way soon cuts left along the head of a slope. After passing between holly hedges the track forks. Turn right and go down a slope, over a stream draining a pond, then up to brick outbuildings at Twyford Farm. (Grid ref: 396311)

Coming onto the farm drive turn right, and after passing through a gate join another drive coming from Twyford Lodge. Veer left, and in a few paces cross the greensward on the right on a narrow path. This leads into woodland and scrub. After a few yards come to a crossing path. Bear left then immediately right on a narrow continuing path which eventually leads to a narrow lane. Turn right downhill, soon passing a house on the right. Down the slope cut right on a footpath into woodland. Twisting through the woods cross a footbridge over a stream, and come onto the lane once more. Across this the continuing path slants rampwise up the slope among conifers, and after gaining a high point it then slopes down a little to rejoin the lane at a minor crossroads. (Grid ref: 401303)

Walk directly ahead (direction Birch Grove and Horsted Keynes) and in a few paces take a path on the right. Returning to woodland this soon leads alongside a garden boundary and emerges to the head of a drive near a group of houses. Turn sharp right, pass a barn and walk down a slope, then through a gate maintain direction among lovely beech trees. At the foot of the slope do not go onto the lane, but turn hard left along a bridleway. This soon takes you above the first of a series of small lakes or ponds, and becomes a track (muddy in winter). Ignore alternatives to right and left and keep to the main bridleway/track through Birchgrove Wood. When at last you emerge from the woods the way cuts left and rises to Birchgrove Road. (Grid ref: 394292)

Turn right for 450yds, then bear right on a concrete drive leading to Horsted Keynes Reservoir. In a few yards break off on a footpath going ahead. Soon come to a metal kissing gate on the left. At this point the Main Walk heads directly for the centre of the village, while those on route A who need to return to the Bluebell Railway (2) continue ahead towards the church. (See below for details.) To return to the village go through the gate and follow the path as it strikes through two meadows, then edges a third (all linked by kissing gates). Across this last meadow the path skirts alongside allotments, comes to the Village Hall, then goes along the drive to reach the main road. Turn right to reach the Post Office where the walk began.

Route A: Do not go through the kissing gate but continue ahead on a clear path leading to Horsted Keynes church. Bear left along Church Lane to reach the path on the right used on the outward route from the station. Retrace this route back to the Bluebell Railway.

Items of interest:

1: Horsted Keynes has an attractive and well-tended village green, two pubs, some Tudor houses and a Norman church reached by a lane between timber-framed or tile-hung cottages. The church has a 13th century tower, and former Prime Minister, Harold Macmillan, is buried in the churchyard. North of the village the string of lakes once powered the hammers of local iron-masters. Nearby Cinder Hill is said to derive its name from the cinder and slag taken from the ironworkers' furnaces.

2: The Bluebell Railway owes its existence to the enthusiasts of a Preservation Society who bought the track and rolling stock from British Rail after the East Grinstead to Lewes line was closed in 1958. Three years later the 5-mile stretch between Sheffield Park and Horsted Keynes was reopened. This original Bluebell Line has since been extended north as far as Kingscote Station, and this is linked with East Grinstead mainline services by vintage bus. The Bluebell Railway was named after the bluebell woods through which the line passes.

WALK 14
Balcombe - Ardingly Reservoir - Balcombe

Distance:	7½ miles (or 7¼ miles by route A option)
Map:	OS Explorer 135 (18) 'Ashdown Forest' 1:25,000
Start:	Balcombe Victory Hall & Social Club (Grid ref: 309306)
Access:	By rail on the London-Brighton line (Balcombe Station). By road, off B2036 about 5 miles south-east of Crawley.
Parking:	With discretion in the village.
Refreshments:	Ardingly Reservoir Activity Centre, summer and bank holidays only. Pubs and tearoom in Balcombe.

This is a truly splendid walk, one of the most attractive and interesting in this book. It begins by heading south out of Balcombe, through woodland and onto a hilltop crown with broad vistas typical of the High Weald. Then down to little streams that drain through a shallow valley before heading east to pass beneath the Ouse Valley Viaduct that carries the London-Brighton railway line. This is an astonishing piece of architecture when seen in profile, and is no less fascinating when viewed from the archways themselves. Beyond the viaduct the walk follows the modest River Ouse for a while, then joins the shoreline path round the eastern side of Ardingly Reservoir, home to ducks and geese and great crested grebe, on a good path that eventually leads back to Balcombe via Balcombe Lake, with a slightly shorter return option. Take a picnic lunch and give a whole day to the walk. You'll not regret it.

*   *   *

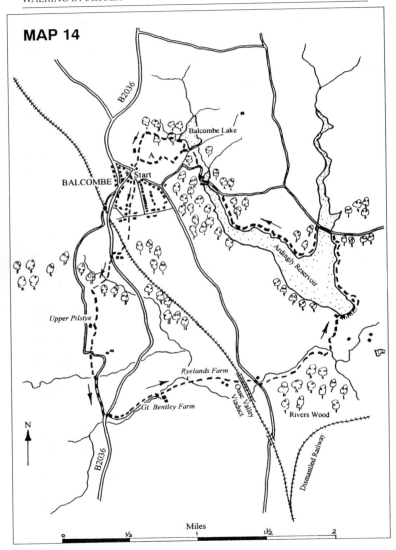

MAP 14

Balcombe Lake

A

BALCOMBE

Start

B2036

Ardingly Reservoir

Upper Pilstye

Ryelands Farm

Ouse Valley Viaduct

Gt. Bentley Farm

Rivers Wood

N

Dismantled Railway

B2036

Miles

½   1   1½   2

The walk begins in the heart of Balcombe (1) by the Victory Hall which stands beside a minor road near the Post Office. With the hall entrance on your right walk ahead for a few yards to find a tarmac path on the right which leads into the village playing field. Skirt the left-hand edge and come to a residential street. Continue ahead. At a crossing road maintain direction through a meadow with woodland on the left, then among scrub to the railway line. Cross this with care and shortly after come onto the drive of Kemps House which is followed as far as the main B2036. (Grid ref: 307296) *then thru a gate*

Cross the road, turn left and about 100 yards later go over a stile on the right with a path sloping down along the edge of a small woodland into a meadow. Across this an oak post guides the way to Pilstye Wood which is entered by another stile and a footbridge. This is a pleasant wood with open sections bright with bluebells and wild garlic, and later with rhododendrons and orchids. At a junction of tracks take the upper branch to pass a rock outcrop overhung with beech trees. Come onto a hilltop with far-reaching views that include a hint of the South Downs, and a brief glimpse of the Ouse Valley Viaduct ahead to the left. The path now slopes down to the south, passing to the left of a solitary house called Upper Pilstye. (Grid ref: 304287)

Below the house cross a small meadow and continue between a series of fields with the 17th century Pilstye Farm seen to the left, and come to a very narrow lane. Cross this slightly left ahead, and continue down the edge of a field to rejoin the lane where it crosses the Upper Ouse stream. Walk along the lane for about a third of a mile to its junction with the B2036, then bear sharp left for a few paces before crossing the road and walking along a drive towards Great Bentley Farm. On the final approach to the farm the drive curves right and crosses a brook. A few paces beyond this cross a stile on the left into a long meadow. Walk along the right-hand boundary, and when the hedgerow cuts back to the right continue ahead to cross a sturdy footbridge over the River Ouse. (Grid ref: 315280) Off to the right can be seen the remarkable Ouse Valley Viaduct (2).

Across the bridge the path continues half-right to a stile beside a field gate. Walk up a sloping meadow to its top right-hand corner, cross a pair of stiles and continue towards Ryelands Farm. Follow the drive to the farm, then curve left and soon go over a stile on the right to gain an impressive view of the viaduct with its 37 red brick arches spanning the valley. The footpath leads through the left-hand archway where it's worth pausing for a moment or two to gaze along the tall oval spaces between the brick pillars to gain a very unusual architectural impression. Through the viaduct keep ahead to a country road, then bear right. Almost immediately after crossing the River Ouse again join a footpath on the left. (Grid ref: 325280)

The path accompanies this stream for a little over half a mile through gentle meadowland and alongside River's Wood. At the far end of the meadow cross an arched footbridge over the stream, followed by a second footbridge a few paces later. Walk up the right-hand side of a field, and near the crown of the hill go through a gap on the right and along the right-hand boundary of the adjacent field. From the gap the Ouse Valley Viaduct is once more seen arching across the valley, while from the next field the expansive buildings of Ardingly College (3) dominate the view until Ardingly Reservoir (4) appears ahead. The way leads directly to the southern end of the reservoir near the Activity Centre. (Grid ref: 334287) Refreshments are available here at certain times of the year.

Cross the grass-banked dam and then walk along the shoreline footpath on the eastern side of the reservoir. In its early stages this path is part of the 'Kingfisher Trail' - a nature trail with numbered posts indicating sites of interest. An interpretation leaflet is currently available from the bird hide situated among trees on the left of the trail. (Grid ref: 335289)

As you wander along the shoreline path good views are had across the reservoir, and to the north, where low wooded hills rise from the water broken here and there with open meadows. There's plenty of birdlife in and around the reservoir, and the walk round it is most enjoyable. On coming to a narrow road bear left, cross the causeway and rejoin the shoreline path on the far side where the walk continues for another mile and a half to the head of the reservoir's north-western spur. Here you come onto the road again, bear left and wander downhill to pass The Old Mill on the left and The Mill House on the right. A short way beyond these houses the road curves leftwards. Walking round this you come to a footpath cutting off to the right into trees. (Grid ref: 317306)

Through the trees emerge into a meadow and walk ahead along its right-hand edge beside Alder Wood. Go through to a second meadow, on the far side of which you come to a narrow lane at the southern end of Balcombe Lake. Cross the lane into a small meadow, and ahead to a stile and a field gate with a larger sloping field beyond where there's a junction of paths, both of which lead back to Balcombe. (Grid ref: 315308)

Route A: Walk uphill along the left-hand boundary, and at the top of the slope bear left alongside a boundary hedge. A stile in the field corner provides access to a footpath which soon enters Balcombe's cricket ground. Walk round the right-hand boundary to a hedge-lined track that leads directly to the village by The Half Moon Inn.

Main walk contd: Bear right round the lower boundary to rejoin the lake in an attractive wooded area. The path rises above the lake and into a small meadow, across which you enter Walk Wood. There are several footbridges within this wood as the path leads through. Bear left at all junctions and so emerge to a final hilltop meadow affording more lovely views over a peaceful countryside almost devoid of buildings. Pass the large Balcombe House on your right and come onto a track/driveway (shared by Route A). Bear right and shortly come to The Half Moon Inn. Cross the road to the Post Office. For the railway station continue ahead, while the Victory Hall and Social Club is in the road on the left.

Items of interest:

1: Balcombe has a number of listed buildings, several of which are roofed with Horsham slabs. The name means 'evil valley', or 'valley of dread'.

2: The Ouse Valley Viaduct was built between 1839-1841 at a cost of £38,500, and was designed by David Moccatto, architect for Brighton Station. The viaduct is 1475 feet long, 96 feet high at its loftiest point, with 37 arches, each spanning 30 feet. In order to limit the number of bricks required to build it, the piers were broken by elegant oval spaces. It is said that the viaduct used more than 11 million bricks in its construction. Although the River Ouse today is

91

little more than a modest stream where it flows beneath the viaduct, it was a navigable waterway in the 19th century, and building materials used in the viaduct's construction were brought to the site by river.

3: Ardingly College was founded in 1858 by Nathaniel Woodard to provide 'comprehensive and classless' education. The main red brick buildings which form two courtyards were opened in 1870.

4: Ardingly Reservoir was created in 1978, and is managed by South East Water to serve customers in mid-Sussex, and as far afield as Crowborough and Hailsham. It covers an area of 193 acres (78 hectares) and holds a maximum of 1047 million gallons (4773m litres) of water. Its maximum depth is 46 feet (14m). In addition to its use for water storage, the reservoir is popular for sailing, angling and birdwatching. There's a hide at the south-eastern end that is open for public access.

WALK 15
Slaugham - Warninglid - Slaugham

Distance:	5 miles
Map:	OS Explorer 134 'Crawley & Horsham' 1:25,000
Start:	Slaugham Common (Grid ref: 251281)
Access:	By way of minor roads off B2110 or A23, 1¹/₂ miles southwest of Handcross.
Parking:	On north side of crossroads, by Furnace Pond. (Grid ref: 251281)
Refreshments:	Pub in Warninglid

Though situated only a few fields west of the thunderous A23, both Slaugham and Warninglid are remarkably tranquil villages, to all intents and purposes preserved in a landscape not yet threatened by tarmac or concrete. Researching this walk we watched deer, rabbit and heron, feasted on blackberries and were serenaded by birdsong while 747s climbed steeply from unseen Gatwick, the roar of their engines no more than a distant purr that did little to disturb the rural peace. It's a walk that explores heart-of-Sussex farmland, with meadows and woods rolling gently to blue horizons. Slaugham church is charming and worth a brief visit, while the lake below

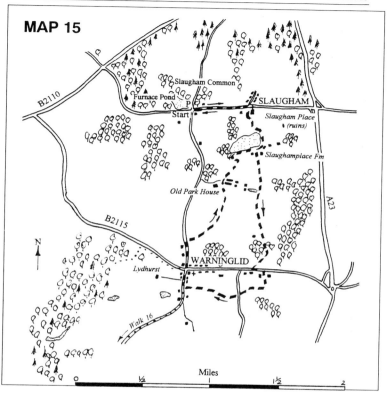

MAP 15

B2110

Furnace Pond

Slaugham Common

P

Start

SLAUGHAM

Slaugham Place (ruins)

Slaughamplace Fm

Old Park House

B2115

A23

N

WARNINGLID

Lydhurst

Walk 16

Miles

0 ½ 1 1½ 2

invites rest. The pub at Warninglid comes at the midway point, and for the extra-energetic there's an opportunity to extend the walk here by combining this route with that of Walk 16.

* * *

The parking area in Coos Lane on the northern side of the crossroads at Slaugham Common overlooks Furnace Pond where ducks squabble for titbits and anglers spend patient hours waiting for a bite. Turn left (east) and walk along the road into Slaugham - pronounced Slaffem (1). Enter the churchyard, and when the path

Furnace Pond at Slaugham Common

forks go ahead, soon wandering along the right-hand edge of a field across which can be seen the ruins of Slaugham Place. The way goes through a small woodland, along the eastern end of a lake and onto a drive where you bear right. Remain on the drive until it ends by the entrance to Slaughamplace Farm, then continue ahead on a hedge-lined path. Over a stile maintain direction along the left-hand edge of a meadow, then between wooden fences to reach the end of another lake - unmarked on the OS map.(Grid ref: 258271)

Passing this to your right continue ahead along the left-hand side of a large field, and when you've gone beyond a projecting line of trees make for a point midway between the top left-hand corner and a low brick-built barn. A signpost directs the path here into a wood. Rising among trees the path leaves the wood at its top left-hand corner where a stile delivers you into a hilltop field. Cross half-right to locate another stile in the opposite boundary hedge a short distance left of a gate. Turn left along Cuckfield Lane, and after about 200 yards bear right on the drive to Southgate Farm. Through a gate by a cattle grid continue slightly right ahead alongside stables, then on a concrete drive. When this curves left, go through a gate ahead and cross a stile on the right. The way now leads along the left-hand edge of a series of paddocks linked by stiles, then you veer left after crossing a footbridge, walk across an enclosed field to its top left-hand corner and out to a lane. (Grid ref: 256258)

Bear left for a few paces, then into a field on the right where you walk directly ahead, through a kissing gate and ahead among laurel and holly to a second kissing gate. Maintain direction along the edge of another field, with a pond seen at the foot of the slope. A third kissing gate takes the path into another laurel grove, beyond which you follow the left-hand edge of a field, go alongside allotments and emerge in The Street in Warninglid. (2) (Grid ref: 250257)

Note: Should you wish to extend the walk and link this with the 4-mile circuit described as Walk 16, turn left at this point and wander down the lane, passing the former Rifleman pub at the bottom of the hill. The rest of the Warninglid-Minepits Wood-Warninglid walk should then be followed as far as The Half Moon pub at Warninglid crossroads (Grid ref: 250261) where you rejoin the Main Walk for the return to Slaugham.

Main Walk contd: Turn right and wander along The Street, passing some attractive tile-hung houses and a couple of pretty ponds by the drive to the Lydhurst Estate, beyond which you come to crossroads and The Half Moon pub. Cross directly ahead into Slaugham Lane. After about 350 yards a kissing gate on the right leads into a large field where a path makes for the far left-hand corner. Go through a gap into a small enclosed field, out through another gap and ahead a few paces. Now bear left over a stile onto a path alongside a fence. (This can be somewhat overgrown in full summer.) Ahead can be seen Old Park House, while the path leads to, and between, some barns and over a stile on the north side of these. Walk across the field to its right-hand corner where you'll find a double stile by an oak tree. From here bear left and wander round the edge of the next field, until you come to another stile by a large oak on the left. Over this the path now leads parallel to a lake - with a few access points between trees to the shoreline. At the end of the lake come to a farm drive, bear left, and shortly after head left on a footpath along the eastern end of the lake. This should be familiar as it was used on the outward route. Going first through a patch of woodland, it then eases up to Slaugham church and the road. Bear left for the car park at Slaugham Common.

Items of interest:

1: Slaugham is a tiny village whose attractive cottages face one another across a dead-end street leading away from the church. The Church of St Mary dates from Norman times. Although much restored in the 19th century, it retains its 13th century tower, and among the various memorials is a splendidly carved monument to Richard Covert whose family kneels in prayer behind him - all 17 of them, picked out in stone. Below and to the south-east stand the remains of Slaugham Place, a large Elizabethan manor and one-time home of the Coverts. Sir Robert, who built the house, was High Sheriff of Sussex and several times an MP. His house was originally surrounded by a turreted wall within 700 acres of deer park, which included the large lake whose shoreline is visited on the walk. One authority says that under Sir Robert Slaugham Place was staffed by 70 servants. After the house was abandoned its oak staircase was removed and it now adorns Lewes Town Hall.

2: Warninglid is no bigger than Slaugham, but it boasts a pub and, among the neat tile-hung houses of The Street, a pair of tiny ponds guarding the entrance to a drive leading to the Lydhurst Estate. Before he became famous, Tennyson lived in the village.

WALK 16
Warninglid - Minepits Wood - Warninglid

Distance:	4 miles
Map:	OS Explorer 134 'Crawley & Horsham' 1:25,000
Start:	Warninglid crossroads (Grid ref: 250261)
Access:	Via B2115 1¼ miles west of Pitts Head Crossroads on A23.
Parking:	With consideration in the village.
Refreshments:	The Half Moon pub, Warninglid.

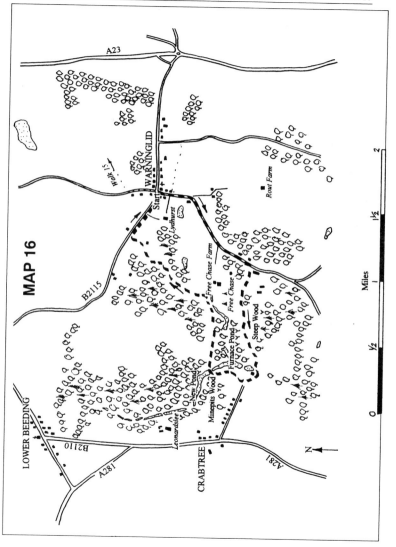

MAP 16

A23

WARNINGLID

Walk 15

Start

Lydhurst

Rout Farm

B2115

Free Chase Farm

Free Chase

Steep Wood

Furnace Pond

New Pond

Leonardslee

Mineputs Wood

LOWER BEEDING

B2110

A281

CRABTREE

A281

N

Miles

0   ½   1   1½   2

Although one of the shortest walks in this book, it's a hilly circuit, and therefore quite strenuous. Much of it is in woodland - very fine woodland at that - and it edges Leonardslee Gardens which are noted for their magnificent rhododendrons and azaleas. There are rhododendrons on this walk too, and whilst they will be colourful in early summer, autumnal tints in the woods can be just as memorable. The first mile is on a country lane, but this is justified as there's very little traffic using it. Thereafter, trees dominate. Keep alert for sight of deer, and for wallabies behind a fence as you skirt the Leonardslee Estate.

*   *   *

From The Half Moon pub at the crossroads walk through Warninglid along The Street, soon sloping downhill and swinging to the right beside the former Rifleman pub. (Ahead a drive leads to Rout Farm and this, linked with footpaths, offers a $2^1/2$ mile alternative to the initial lane section of our walk.) At the entrance to Free Chase Farm the lane curves left, continues between fields, and rises by a woodland section. Immediately before a row of tile-hung houses leave the lane for a footpath on the right. Among trees and laurel bushes the way is led by a fence, and after going through a squeeze stile you come to a path junction. Continue directly ahead, now on a bridleway, but at the next junction leave it in favour of a footpath rising among bracken into Steep Wood. Beneath power lines come to a more open area, but then slope downhill, the path lined with heather, to rejoin the bridleway. Bear right to pass alongside a pond. (Grid ref: 229249)

Beyond the pond go through a gate and up the right-hand edge of a field to a drive. Turn right past 'Gorsedene' and keep on the drive until it forks at the end of Mill Lane - which comes from the A281 at Crabtree. Now turn sharp right and ahead through a possible parking area to enter Minepits Wood. At a junction of tracks note through the fence on the left you can often see wallabies! Walk down the slope, the bridleway soon curving and crossing a causeway between two lakes - the right-hand of these (Furnace Pond) is hidden by a dense growth of trees, the left-hand (New Pond) is behind the fence marking the boundary of the Leonardslee Estate (1). (Grid ref: 228255)

The path rises, and then edges an open field before crossing a small stream where it forks. The bridleway cuts left, but we go ahead on a narrow path up a slope and beneath a power cable. Crossing the southern side of Freechase Hill the path loses a little height with another lake hidden below (you may catch a brief glimpse of water through trees and shrubbery), and then the way is blocked by a gate. Now the path swings left and soon edges another open field, the path flanked by rhododendrons. Entering woods once more cross a hilltop and descend to a path junction. Continue ahead, rising yet again, and before long another field is seen to the right. Go through a kissing gate onto a crossing path and bear right. When this forks a few paces later take the central of three ways, cross a track and through more crowding trees and bushes drop to a dip where there's another path junction. Take the right-hand option, for this will eventually bring you to the B2115 north-west of Warninglid. Do not go onto the road but bear right on the continuing bridleway which runs parallel to it. This crosses a drive to the Lydhurst Estate and soon after joins the road. Wander along this to the crossroads in Warninglid where the walk began.

Items of interest:

1: Leonardslee is noted for its magnificent landscaped garden set in a 240-acre valley with a string of seven lakes which mark one of the principal sources of the River Adur. Begun by Sir Edmund Loder in 1889 (the wallabies are descendants of those introduced by him) the several varieties of rhododendrons and azaleas are perhaps best seen in May, while the woodland trees, especially the maples, are splendid in the autumn. In addition to wallabies, the deer parks contain Fallow, Sika and Axis Deer. The gardens are open daily from the beginning of April until the end of October. (Tel: 01403 891212)

WALK 17
Horsham - Southwater - Horsham

Distance:	7 miles
Map:	OS Explorer 134 'Crawley & Horsham' 1:25,000
Start:	St Mary's Church, Horsham (Grid ref: 171303)
Access:	By train, Horsham is on the Crawley-Littlehampton line.
Parking:	Multi-storey car park north of the church.
Refreshments:	None on the walk, but pubs, cafés and shops in Horsham.

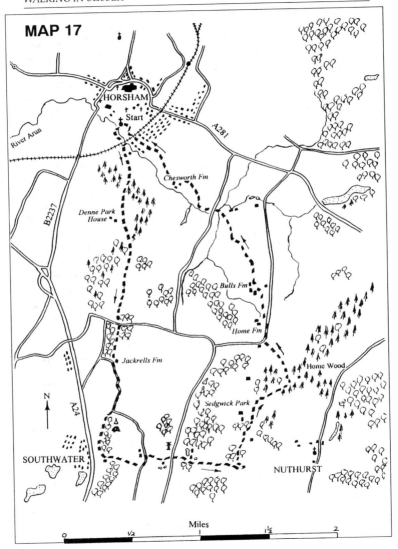

MAP 17

HORSHAM

Start

A281

River Arun

B2237

Chesworth Fm

Denne Park House

Bulls Fm

Home Fm

N

Jackrells Fm

A24

Home Wood

Sedgwick Park

SOUTHWATER

NUTHURST

Miles

0   ½   1   1½   2

South of Horsham gentle wooded hills and meadows suggest a pleasant walking country, and this particular route explores some of the best on offer. Between the A24 to the west and A281 to the east, it's a sparsely-populated landscape cut by modest streams and country lanes that serve isolated farms and handsome country manors. Since our route begins on the very edge of Horsham it takes only a few brief minutes to escape the town, while a return at the end of the walk is surprisingly easy and unfussed. A packed lunch should be carried as there are no refreshment facilities along the way.

*　　*　　*

The elegant spired, 13th century church of St Mary the Virgin is situated at the southern end of Horsham (1), not far from the Sainsbury's store. With your back to the town go round the left-hand side of the church and, passing a Primary School on your left, cross the River Arun and turn left at a crossing path on the edge of a sports ground. The path soon recrosses the Arun by a railway bridge. Through this turn right and walk ahead along a private drive. When it forks bear left, and almost immediately cross a stile on the right. Keep along the left-hand edge of a meadow to the top corner where another stile directs the continuing path between fences. On reaching woods maintain direction uphill, and at the head of the slope emerge to the open expanse of Denne Park. (Grid ref: 171295)

Cross the parkland towards the left-hand side of Denne Park House, where you follow a boundary hedge for about 30 yards before veering slightly left towards another woodland. The way cuts through these woods and joins a bridleway - the Pedlar's Way (2). Follow this ahead, out of the woods. The bridleway becomes a drive by a house, where you continue ahead to a country road. Bear left for a few paces, then take a path on the right through yet another woodland. When this brings you out of the woods maintain direction towards Jackrells Farm. Go through the farmyard to reach a country lane with the South Downs seen in the distance. (Grid ref: 169274)

Bear left. After almost ¹/₂ mile the lane makes a sharp left-hand bend. At this point bear right on a track, then left after a few paces to follow a path alongside a woodland shaw, on the far side of which there's a caravan site. At a junction of paths veer left through a copse, then across a field towards the half-timbered Stakers Farm. Bear left along a track which soon narrows to a fence-enclosed bridleway leading to a country lane - an extension of the lane along which you recently walked. (Grid ref: 172261)

Turn left for a short distance, and on drawing level with Lockyers Farm, cross a stile on the right and walk towards the right-hand end of a barn. Go through a gate into a small field to the left of a house, and wander slightly left ahead to a stile found roughly midway in the opposite hedgerow. Cross Broadwater Lane into a larger field and walk ahead to another stile below an electricity pole. The way then continues through a copse, over a stream and out to a field with a pond on the left. Follow the left-hand boundary, but when this cuts back, maintain direction across the field corner to a track. After about 100 yards this goes through a gap into another field, at the far side of which there's a crossing track where you bear left, then left again - in effect cutting back along a field edge. Soon enter woods where the way veers right on a bridleway. Come to a drive near Lower Sedgwick Farm and walk ahead. (Grid ref: 184264)

Remain on the drive as it rises uphill and passes to the right of the grey stone building of Sedgwick Park. About 40 yards beyond this take a track on the right into Home Wood, soon gaining hinted views between the trees. The woods thin, and about 100 yards before it reaches a house, leave the track to follow a footpath on the left. In a couple of paces veer right. When it forks take the right branch to maintain direction. After tracing the edge of a meadow the way goes through another woodland, which it leaves after crossing a footbridge. Now cross a field towards a white house, North Lodge, and come onto a lane. (Grid ref: 186275)

Bear right, and a few paces after passing the entrance to Home Farm, enter the field on the left and continue ahead alongside the right-hand hedge. When this slants to the right, maintain direction to a stile in the opposite fence. Horsham comes into view as you walk towards it. Over the stile keep ahead, soon walking on a path between hedges to reach a farm drive. Bear left towards Bull's Farm House, then turn right. Cross a stile between a stable and a barn, and go half-left across a field to reach a concrete farm road, where you bear right. Follow the road until it finishes, then continue ahead to the top corner of a field where another stile gives access to a second field. Once again continue in the same direction. In the bottom corner a makeshift stile (during research, that is) leads to yet another field. Halfway along this, cross a stile on the right, then walk down the left-hand edge of a narrow field, near the bottom of which you go through a gate. Near the bottom left-hand corner a footbridge takes you over a stream (the Arun) and onto a drive. Bear left to a road near Amiesmill Bridge. (Grid ref: 181292)

Across the road walk through a field to a line of three oak trees. Bear right, go through a gate, then bear half-left towards the top left-hand corner of another field. There you come to a four-way path junction. Continue ahead along a grass strip between fields to reach a drive by a cream-painted house. Bear right past a pond, and follow the drive as far as a residential street, Chesworth Lane. Maintain direction, and shortly after passing beneath a railway bridge, bear right into Denne Road. Take the first turning on the left, and come to the church of St Mary the Virgin where the walk began.

Items of interest:

1: Horsham is virtually the 'capital' of the western Weald, a prosperous market town that grew from a Saxon settlement built alongside a drover's road where it crossed the River Arun. It was a centre for horse breeding (the name means 'horse meadow'), and its twice weekly market was established during medieval times. From 1306 to 1830 Horsham was one of the principal Sussex assize towns. As a consequence, public executions often took place on the Common. The last public execution held here was in 1844, when a crowd of some 3,000 came to watch as John Lawrence was hanged for the murder of a Brighton policeman. The poet Shelley would have known Horsham well, for he was born (in August 1792) at Field Place near Broadbridge Heath, and it is said that as a child he would sail his boat on Warnham mill pond - now a nature reserve. Thanks to access by rail to both London and the Sussex coast, in recent years Horsham has expanded considerably, but its growth is now restricted to north and west by the A264 and A24 which bypass the town. In his book on the county, published in 1894, Augustus Hare described it as "a very picturesque little country town." It is doubtful whether he would recognise much of Horsham now, yet despite development, a number of notable buildings survive - especially those which line

The Carfax, and The Causeway leading to the church.

2: The Pedlar's Way is a cycling and walking route named after the annual Pedlary Fair that was held during the 18th and 19th centuries in Southwater. The route follows bridleways and minor roads between Horsham and Southwater Country Park.

WALK 18
Shipley - West Grinstead - Shipley

Distance:	6 miles
Maps:	OS Explorer 134 'Crawley & Horsham', and 121 'Arundel & Pulborough' 1:25,000
Start:	Shipley Church (Grid ref: 145218)
Access:	Shipley is reached via a minor road south of A272, about 7 miles south-west of Horsham.
Parking:	Official parking spaces on road near King's Windmill (Grid ref: 144219)
Refreshments:	The Crown pub, and the Pepper Mill restaurant, in Dial Post.

Three small villages, two churches, a windmill, a castle and lake. Add to these ingredients an idyllic 'back-of-beyond' countryside through which the infant River Adur sidles, and a good day's walking is assured. This is Belloc country. The poet who sang the praises of Sussex as loudly as anyone before or since, spent most of his life in Shipley and owned the windmill there for almost fifty years. He too was a wanderer. No doubt he would have trod the footpaths and trackways followed by this route, and the landscape will have changed little since his time. Except, of course, for the speed and volume of traffic on the A24. The fields and meadows have their own pace of life, their own sense of tranquillity, and it is these above all which make this walk so attractive.

*   *   *

From Shipley church (1) walk north through the village along Red Lane, and just beyond the last bungalow on the right go through a kissing gate into a field. Follow the right-hand boundary to a second kissing gate which then leads the path through Church Wood. On

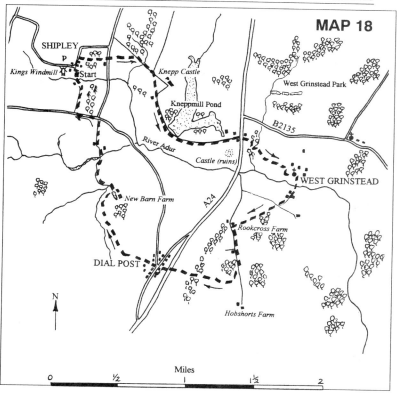

leaving this continue ahead on the edge of another field, and out to a narrow country road by a house. Over the road maintain direction among more trees, then directly across a field to join a drive leading to Knepp Castle (2). Follow the drive a short distance, until a second drive cuts from it to the left. At this point take to the field on the right and make for a large oak tree in the top right-hand corner. There you rejoin the drive and bear right, passing a lodge. (Grid ref: 154215)

Follow the drive/lane all the way to the A24. On the way views show Chanctonbury Ring on the crest of the distant South Downs, and before long you pass along an embankment at the southern end of the extensive Kneppmill Pond - once the largest hammer pond in Sussex. Just before reaching the A24, note the single remaining wall of the Norman Knepp Castle (stronghold of the de Braose family) standing on a grass mound in a field off to the right. At the edge of the A24 note also the coat of arms fixed to a garden wall on the right. (Grid ref: 164211)

Cross the road with great care and enter a field on the eastern side, to the right of a house. Over this field walk directly ahead to a woodland shaw, crossing a stream at its entrance. The path swings to the right, in the shaw, then left along the edge of a field. Remain on the right-hand side of a second field until the boundary cuts back, then continue ahead to the far side to a footpath signpost. Turn right. In 100 yards bear left to enter West Grinstead churchyard (3). Walk through an avenue of variegated holly, then bear right immediately beyond the church and leave the churchyard at the bottom corner through a kissing gate. Follow a slab path between fields to a footbridge over the River Adur (4). (Grid ref: 171206)

Come onto a farm drive by some houses (marked as Butcher's Row on the OS map), and follow this road beyond the houses and between fields as far as a T-junction. (The left-hand drive goes to Clothalls.) Walk straight ahead now through a large field towards a barn seen on the far horizon. The way passes along the edge of a wood and continues to Rookcross Farm. The footpath route enters a field directly opposite the point where you come onto the farm drive, then cuts left, parallel with the drive (Rookcross Lane). During research the field route was very tangled and it was easier to walk along the drive/lane. The footpath rejoins the lane in the bottom left-hand corner of the field near a house, where a second drive breaks away to the right (to Rooklands Farm). Maintain direction along Rookcross Lane, and at the far end of a woodland bear right through a gap into a field (the lane continues to Hobshort's Farm). (Grid ref: 164195)

Follow the left-hand edge of the field to the next corner where you go into a belt of trees to crossing paths. Bear right over a stile and along the right-hand edge of a field. On the far side of this the way edges a wood, then crosses a second stile in the bottom corner, goes over a footbridge into another field. Maintain direction and in the top left-hand corner you gain access to the A24 again. Once more take care as you cross, and on the west side enter a small field. Across this bear left through a gate, and soon after cross a stile on the right, wander along the garden boundary of a house and into the beer garden of The Crown in the village of Dial Post. The official way then goes along the back of some houses on the left, and out to the village street next to the Pepper Mill restaurant. (Grid ref: 154194)

Turn right, then over a stile into a field opposite The Crown. Walk across the field and continue through a gap into a second field beside a house. Maintain direction to enter a third field, and go along the right-hand edge until coming to a solitary oak tree where a stile takes the path into another field on the right. Cross this half-left to a gap in the opposite hedge. Now follow the right-hand hedgerow to a gateway in the far corner, and come onto a crossing track. Bear right and wander along the track to a pond by New Barn Farm. Just after the pond turn left on a crossing farm drive. This leads between fields, and when it forks you take the right-hand option, winding between more fields and passing below a pond to reach Hammer Farm. Remain on the farm drive as far as a junction of lanes at Pound Corner. (Grid ref: 148213)

Turn left, and after about ¼ mile bear right on another farm drive, this one going to Church Farm South. Ahead you have a fine view of King's Windmill (5). At the end of the drive go down the slope to the right of the house, cross the Adur on a footbridge and walk across the field half-left to Shipley churchyard.

Items of interest:

1: Shipley Church was built by the Knights Templar in about 1125 after being given the land by the de Braose family. The square, central tower has fine Norman arches, and in the lovely south porch there stands a curious mooring stone, misshapen by the ropes and chains that once tethered river craft to it. That such a stone should be found here would at first glance seem rather odd, until one realizes that the River Adur, now winding innocently through the field below, was once a much more powerful waterway, and was navigable as far inland as Shipley. In the churchyard lies the composer, John Ireland.

2: Knepp Castle was built in 1809 for Sir Charles Burrell, the man responsible for uniting the two estates of Knepp and West Grinstead in 1831. Knepp Castle was almost completely destroyed by fire in 1904, but was rebuilt to the same design. A half mile or so away, the last remains of the original Knepp Castle, built by William de Braose, stand forlorn in a field - a corner wall of a Norman keep built to guard the Bramber to Horsham road. King John used it as a hunting lodge and, apparently, kept 200 greyhounds there which he used to hunt deer. The Civil War was largely responsible for its destruction, and in 1762 most of the stone that was left was used for building the Horsham to Steyning road.

3: West Grinstead Church is dedicated to St George. Roofed with Horsham slabs, a broach spire bursts from it. A Norman door is found on the south side. The south aisle was added in the 13th century, and the pews are notable for bearing the names of 19th century parish farms and houses painted on them. Sadly, the door is kept locked against vandalism, although details of the keyholder are given in the fine 15th century timber porch. In the churchyard, as you enter from the field, a stone on the right marks the grave of Douglas Arnold, Spitfire Pilot, with a moving poem by John Gillespie Magee etched upon it.

4: The River Adur is met several times on walks included in this book. Rising among the hills of the High Weald, it makes a sinuous journey through West Sussex before finding an outlet at Shoreham. It was once much wider than it is today (see 1 above), with a harbour at Steyning on the northern (inland) side of the Downs. West of Henfield the river has two arms, and it's possible to follow the river bank from Betley Bridge outside Henfield (see Walk 28) all the way to Shoreham.

5: King's Windmill is said to be the last of all the smock mills to be built in Sussex, dating from 1879. For nearly fifty years it was owned by Hilaire Belloc, who lived in the house named King's Land from 1906 until his death in 1953 - a poet who loved Sussex and who, in the words of the memorial over the door, "garnered a harvest of wisdom and sympathy for young and old". The mill has been restored since his death. It is now the largest working windmill in Sussex, and is open to the public on set days in summer. It can be seen from as far away as Chanctonbury Ring on the South Downs.

WALK 19
Rye - Iden - River Rother - Rye

Distance:	7 miles
Map:	OS Explorer 125 'Romney Marsh, Rye & Winchelsea' 1:25,000
Start:	Rye Railway Station (Grid ref: 919206)
Access:	By train on the Ashford-Hastings line. By road: via A259 Hastings-Folkestone, or A268 from Hawkhurst (Tunbridge Wells). Buses from Hastings, Tenterden etc.
Parking:	Many car parks in and around the town.
Refreshments:	Pubs, cafés and shops in Rye; pub and shop in Iden.

Heading north away from the historic and ever-popular little town of Rye, the walk explores woods, fields and meadows that flow over gentle hills commanding views across a peaceful land. The turning point is at Iden, a small village astride a crossroads, its recreation ground beside the church providing a restful site for a picnic, while the village pub offers welcome refreshment. From here a series of field paths lead eastward, culminating in a surprise descent through woods, of cliffs that once held back the sea. That sea was pushed back long ago and the flat, sheep-grazed land that replaces it is edged by the River Rother. The return to Rye follows the left bank of this major Sussex river that is tidal for much of the way, and the walk ends among the narrow streets of town.

*   *   *

Coming out of Rye Station turn right, and right again at a T-junction to cross the railway line at a level crossing. The Queen Adelaide pub is just ahead and you walk along a footpath which cuts alongside it, passing along the back of houses and with a school on your right. Beyond the last houses the tarmac path traces an embankment between two streams, and when it curves to the right, leave it by crossing a stile on the left and then follow a grass path beside the little River Tillingham. The meadow through which the path leads is used as a campsite; ahead stands Rolvendene Farm. (Grid ref: 916210)

Cross a stile in front of the farmhouse and go up the right-hand

MAP 19

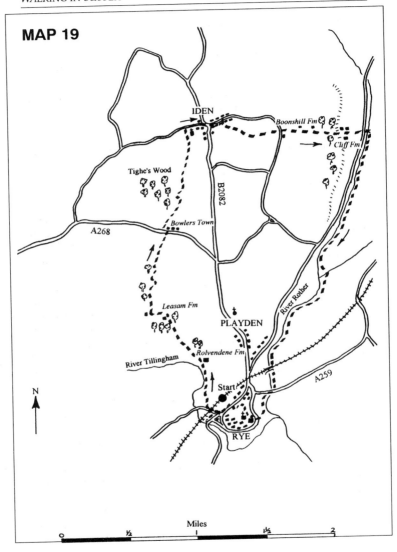

IDEN

Boonshill Fm

Cliff Fm

Tighe's Wood

B2082

Bowlers Town

A268

River Rother

Leasam Fm

PLAYDEN

Rolvendene Fm

River Tillingham

A259

N

Start

RYE

Miles

0   ½   1   1½   2

side of a sloping meadow which leads onto Leasam Hill. Looking back the Tillingham river makes a large bow through the meadows, while Rye lies hunched to the south-east. The way continues over the brow of the hill, and on the far side of the hilltop field goes through a kissing gate onto a drive where there's a choice of routes. Ours continues ahead through a small woodland and emerges onto an unmade farm road which leads directly to Leasam Farm. Bear left immediately beyond the farm, and the track will take you to a converted oasthouse. Here you turn sharp right and continue along the side of Leasam Oast Cottage. Just before the track enters a field take a sunken path which slopes downhill slightly left ahead. Remain on this path as it veers right and eventually spills into a field. Keep to the left-hand boundary and maintain direction, soon rising uphill with the few houses of Bowlers Town seen ahead. (Grid ref: 913227)

On coming to the A268 opposite some white weatherboarded cottages, cross the road, turn left and a few paces later bear right along the right-hand edge of a field. At the end of this maintain direction, and on the far side of the second field cross a metal stile, then go round the left-hand edge of a third field flanked by Tighe's Wood. About 30 yards from the top of the field cross a stile on the left and aim well to the left of a bungalow, where you come onto a crossing farm track. Over this the continuing path leads through a succession of linking fields with Iden church tower seen directly ahead. (One of the fields has been adopted as part of a conservation project, and has been sown with a natural mix of Wealden wild flowers.) The way leads directly into the recreation ground next to the Parish Church of All Saints, Iden, which dates from the 11th century. (Grid ref: 915238)

Turn right on the road which leads to the centre of Iden village at a staggered crossroads. There is a small food store, and The Bell Inn stands on the right. Cross the main road by the pub and walk ahead along Grove Lane (direction Houghton Green and Appledore). On reaching the fourth bungalow on the right take the footpath which leads alongside it, then over a stile into a field where you bear half-left. Another stile in the opposite hedge takes you into an adjacent field where you maintain direction. Passing through a gap in the hedgerow on the far side, walk along the left-hand field

Honeysuckle-filled hedgerow near Iden

boundary, now heading east. When you reach a corner with another path on the left, continue directly ahead towards oasthouses. These stand beside Houghton Lane. (Grid ref: 926237)

Cross the lane and wander along the unmade drive of Boonshill Farm. In late spring this is flanked by dog roses and honeysuckle. Just beyond Boonshill Farm the track curves into a field. Immediately before it does so go ahead on a narrow footpath overhung with hedgerows and trees. This becomes an enchanting sunken path plunging down vegetated cliffs, crossing several footbridges and edging outcrops of rock until at the foot of the cliffs you come to Spring Farm, then Cliff Farm (B&B). Wander ahead on their drive to a road running beside the River Rother. (Grid ref: 936237)

Over the road cross Boonshill Bridge spanning the river, then turn right and follow the left bank, now on the route of both the Saxon Shore Way (1) and Sussex Border Path (2). In a little over a half mile you pass a cottage, then a lock, beyond which the river is tidal. Beyond this the Union Channel enters the Rother, and a grass-covered bridge enables you to cross. Almost a mile later the river is crossed by the railway, and here the path ducks beneath the bridge, then goes up onto an embankment above a row of houses. Just ahead a bridge carries the A259 across to Rye (3). Cross this to the right bank, and on coming to a large open grass area, veer left on a footpath parallel with the quay where fishing boats unload their catches. This brings you onto Fishmarket Road opposite a flight of steps leading up to Ypres Castle Inn. At the top of the steps stands Ypres Tower (4) with a cannon-guarded lookout, and beyond the Tower, the Parish Church of St Mary the Virgin (5). (Grid ref: 922203)

Pass along the right-hand side of the church on a charming cobbled street. Turn left at the end, then right, and at the road which crosses the bottom of this, bear left again. Turn right into Market Road, and you will soon arrive back at the town's railway station.

Items of interest:

1: The Saxon Shore Way is a 163-mile long distance footpath which begins on the south bank of the Thames at Gravesend in Kent and, following the county's coastline, links a series of Roman fortifications built as a defence against Saxon raiding parties, before ending at Hastings in East Sussex. (See *The Saxon Shore Way* by Bea Cowan, Aurum Press.)

2: The Sussex Border Path is met at various times on walks included in this book. It measures some 150 miles on its way round the county boundary between Emsworth and Rye. A shorter alternative to the main Border Path traces the present border between East and West Sussex, breaking away from the main route at East Grinstead and heading south to Brighton.

3: Rye was an important fishing town and port in the Middle Ages when it was girdled on three sides by the sea. It had a large merchant fleet and was an early member of the Confederation of Cinque Ports, but suffered a number of attacks by French raiders against whom it was fortified in the 14th century. In 1377 the French sacked the town and destroyed all its timber buildings. Today Rye is invaded by more friendly visitors, drawn by the many attractive streets lined by a range of charming buildings, among them the 18th century Lamb House, one-time home of novelist Henry James.

4: Ypres Tower dates from the middle of the 13th century, when it was built to defend the town. In those days it was known as Baddings Tower, but having been sold to John de Ypres in 1430 it gained its present name. In 1518 it was used as the town gaol, but it now contains a museum.

5: The Church of St Mary the Virgin is a large building dating from the 12th century, whose most famous feature is the clock, which is said to be the oldest in England still using the original works. There is much of interest in the church, and it's worth spending time at the end of the walk to explore it. On occasion the tower is open to the public, and from it there's a good view across the marshes to Rye harbour.

WALK 20
Robertsbridge - Bodiam Castle - Robertsbridge

Distance:	7¼ miles
Map:	OS Explorer 136 'The Weald' 1:25,000
Start:	Northbridge Street, Robertsbridge (Grid ref: 738239). If parking at Bodiam Castle, begin the walk there.
Access:	By train on the Tunbridge Wells-Hastings line. By road turn west off A21 two miles south of Hurst Green. By bus from Battle and Hawkhurst.
Parking:	At entrance to Robertsbridge Recreation Ground (Grid ref: 738238), beside A21 north side of roundabout (Grid ref: 740243), or at Bodiam Castle (Grid ref: 784255).
Refreshments:	Pubs and shops in Robertsbridge, pub, tearoom and restaurant in Bodiam.

Forbidding Bodiam Castle, rising out of its moat, is one of the most impressive sights in East Sussex. On this walk we approach it alongside a modest stream which, in medieval times, was a much larger, navigable, river thought to be a possible route of invasion by the French during the Hundred Years War. Hence the construction of this massive fortress. The fertile valley of the Rother through which the route makes an elongated circuit, is calm and tranquil, with low wooded hills rising to north and south. Oasthouses punctuate views with their white conical tips, suggesting

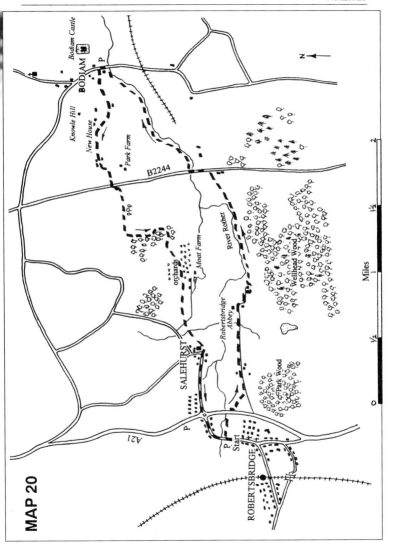

MAP 20

Bodiam Castle

P

BODIAM

Knowle Hill

New House

Park Farm

B2244

River Rother

orchards

Moat Farm

Wellhead Wood

Robertsbridge Abbey

SALEHURST

Park Wood

A21

P

P

Start

ROBERTSBRIDGE

N

Miles

115

Bodiam Castle

that this was once a major hop-growing region. Times change and the extent of Wealden hop-culture has been drastically reduced, in Kent as in Sussex. But there are still a few hop gardens left along this walk, and a group of orchards too. There are also sheep-grazed meadows, large fields of arable land, and plenty of woodlands so typical of the Wealden landscape.

It would be worth allowing sufficient time to visit Bodiam Castle, either before, during or after the walk. Although there is free access to the grounds, the Castle itself is open to the fee-paying public by the National Trust, which has a large car park below it. Should you plan to explore the Castle before or after the walk, it would be better to park here and start the walk at this point.

* * *

The route begins about 100 yards north of the Robertsbridge Recreation Ground car park, where a stile on the right of the road gives access to a meadow with two minor streams cutting through it. Walk directly ahead towards the A21 to a second stile leading the path up to the road, which you cross with care, then enter another meadow and bear half-right, over a concrete bridge and along a drive to Fair Lane. Turn left. When the lane forks by an oasthouse continue directly ahead (now a private road but with bridleway and footpath access), and where other paths break away left towards Salehurst church (1), ignore these and soon you will come to a house on a sharp bend. Note that the west wall of the house has a tall arched window with an ecclesiastical appearance, while the garden is adorned with the remains of the refectory of Robertsbridge Abbey (2). (Grid ref: 755238) On the right-hand side of the lane stands a converted oasthouse.

The lane curves right then left, and soon after, at a gate across the lane, you turn right on a permissive footpath neatly led by fences round the outer garden boundary of a house. When the path comes onto a concrete farm road bear left, then right on the continuing path. This soon enters a field corner where you wander ahead along the left-hand edge. At a path junction in the next corner go up some wooden steps onto a bank above the River Rother, and wander downstream along the bank (this can be somewhat tangled in high summer). When the Rother turns northward the path cuts away from the river bank and heads across a field towards some cottages, coming onto the B2244 road about 100 yards to their left. (Grid ref: 771242)

Turn left for about 200 yards, and immediately after crossing the River Rother, bear right onto the riverside footpath which you follow now all the way to the road a little below Bodiam Castle (3) which soon comes into view. On the opposite bank of the river there's the last remaining stretch of the former Kent and East Sussex Railway (4). Come onto the road at a red-brick bridge and walk up the road to the entrance to Bodiam Castle. (Grid ref:784255) A diversion to walk round the Castle grounds is recommended. At the car park entrance the National Trust has tearooms, while other refreshments are available along the road at The Castle pub, and a restaurant just beyond.

Resuming the walk bear left immediately beyond The Castle on a drive leading between the pub and the village green. This continues beyond the playing fields, and after passing a brick and thatch building, it narrows. Ignore alternative tracks cutting from it and eventually come to a grain store and a complex of large buildings, the last of which is known as Ruskin House. About 100 yards beyond Ruskin House bear left on a footpath alongside a fence, go over a footbridge and through an area of trees and scrub to reach a field by a stile. Bear right, and when the boundary cuts back, maintain direction to a gate and a stile giving onto the B2244 again. (Grid ref: 769253)

Directly ahead another stile leads into a field. Walk along the bottom left-hand boundary, then swing right, still in the field, to the top corner and another stile. Over this a large field is crossed heading in the same direction. In the middle of this a group of trees hides a pond. Pass along the right-hand side of the trees and continue to the far boundary. There you will find another stile in a narrow gap. Do not cross, but remain in the field and walk down the edge, soon alongside a wood. Near the bottom of the slope bear right to pass among trees. Cross a footbridge over a stream and maintain direction, still among trees, walking now up a gentle slope in a long woodland shaw. Up the slope the way swings left for a few paces, then over a stile enters a field corner. (Grid ref: 764246)

Bear left and at the next corner enter an orchard. Maintain direction through two sections of this orchard, and at the bottom edge bear right for about 40 yards before passing into another section of orchard on the left. Walk up the slope following a line of posts. Out of the orchard go down a slope towards Moat Farm for about 45 yards, then bear right, cross a stile by a gate and walk directly ahead across a sloping field with a Dutch barn below. Salehurst church tower can be seen ahead. The way continues through the next field, and on reaching the far corner, go through a gap onto a track, turn right and almost immediately bear left into a final field. Keep to the right-hand edge, and at the top corner bear left for a few paces before a gap gives access to Salehurst churchyard. It is worth giving a few minutes to explore the church, which is a large and interesting building. (Grid ref: 749241)

Out of the church walk ahead along Church Road, past The Salehurst Halt pub, a reminder of the days when the Kent and East Sussex Railway served the village. The road leads directly to the A21. Cross this just to the right of the roundabout, then go ahead along Northbridge Street into Robertsbridge, passing on the way the New Eight Bells pub on the right.

Items of interest:

1: Salehurst church, dedicated to St Mary, is much larger than would be expected for such a small village, even though it serves Robertsbridge as well. It was begun in the thirteenth century, and enlarged in the fourteenth by the monks of Robertsbridge Abbey. One of the most interesting features is the font, placed just inside the entrance. This is said to have been given by Richard Coeur de Lion, and is cleverly decorated with salamanders.

2: Robertsbridge Abbey was founded in 1176 by Cistercian monks, for whom it was originally built on the north side of the Rother at Salehurst by Robert de St Martin. By 1220 it was one of the three great religious houses of Sussex (the others being Battle and Lewes). However, at the time of the dissolution in 1538, there were only eight monks left. Few remnants are to be seen today, although it is supposed that the original Abbey Farm building housed the abbot.

3: Bodiam Castle was built in 1385 by Sir Edward Dalyngrygge as a defence against possible attack by the French who, it was feared, would penetrate this far inland via the Rother. Eight years earlier the French fleet had sacked and burnt the port of Rye, and the Hundred Years' War was still actively being played out on land and sea. Dalyngrygge had gained a licence to "strengthen and crenellate" his manor house. But Bodiam Castle was no addition to an existing building, rather it was a purpose-built fortress that, as luck would have it, was never put to the test, although it was occupied by the Yorkists in 1483. Emerging from a moat on a rise above the river, it is a romantic setting for such a grim and sturdy castle.

4: The Kent and East Sussex Railway ran between Robertsbridge and Tenterden, and was heavily used in the summer by hop-pickers. It was closed by BR in 1961. The eastern end of the line is gradually being reclaimed and restored by volunteer enthusiasts who currently operate a steam service between Tenterden and Northiam. There are plans to eventually reopen the complete line to Robertsbridge. Enquiries to K&ESR, Tenterden Town Station, Tenterden, Kent TN30 6HE (Tel. 01580 765155)

WALK 21
Burwash - Franchise Manor - Batemans - Burwash

Distance:	5 miles
Map:	OS Explorer 136 'The Weald' 1:25,000
Start:	The Bear Inn, Burwash (Grid ref: 675247)
Access:	By bus from Heathfield or Battle. Burwash is on A265 four miles northeast of Heathfield.
Parking:	Public car park (with toilets) behind The Bear Inn on south side of Burwash High Street. (Grid ref: 675247)
Refreshments:	Pubs, shops, restaurant and tearooms in Burwash.

Straggling along a ridge between the valleys of the Rother and the Dudwell, the delightfully attractive village of Burwash was once a centre of the Wealden iron industry. Three centuries later it is better known for being Rudyard Kipling's home. On this walk we explore both the Rother's valley and that of the Dudwell, and wander past Kipling's mansion, Bateman's, which is now in the care of the National Trust. It's a walk with pleasures in every half-mile.

* * *

Cross to the north side of Burwash (1) High Street opposite The Bear Inn and turn right. Just beyond the Post Office turn left down a narrow lane to pass The Rose and Crown pub and continue along a track which soon eases between fields with open views. This curves slightly left to slope gently downhill - ignore the path off to the right. Approaching a solitary house the track curves right then left, and on the bend you cross a stile on the left, and another a few paces beyond, and wander across an open sloping field. Honeybrook Wood makes a right-angle round this field and on the far side you enter the woodland by a stile. The path twists among trees, and emerges on the west side where you turn right to cut across a corner to yet another stile beside a field gate. With a large field now stretching ahead walk along the left-hand edge beside a small stream marked as Seller's Brook on the OS map. Halfway along go through a gap on the left and enter the adjacent field where you have a choice of footpaths. (Grid ref: 669259)

Keep to the left-hand boundary hedge, and at the top corner

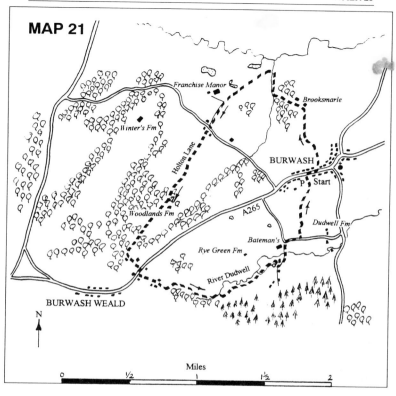

MAP 21

Franchise Manor

Brooksmarle

Winter's Fm

Holton Lane

BURWASH

P Start

Woodlands Fm

A265

Dudwell Fm

Bateman's

Rye Green Fm

River Dudwell

BURWASH WEALD

N

Miles

0   ½   1   1½   2

maintain direction up a gentle slope with lovely countryside spreading off to the right, while Burwash can be seen to the left. Soon you'll find yourself walking parallel to a fence enclosing the park-like grounds of Franchise Manor - an austere grey stone building spied between trees to the right. Just beyond a field gate, cross a stile on the right to join the drive leading from the manor and its farm. Bear left on the drive as far as a narrow road, passing on the way a simple memorial to a young airman killed in action in 1940. The road, Spring Lane, is reached opposite Holton Farm. (Grid ref: 662252)

Bear left for a few paces, then turn right on a narrow bridleway cutting alongside the farm's hedge boundary. Do not take the path which breaks off to the right shortly after, but continue ahead on the bridleway which soon becomes a hedge-lined track known as Holton Lane. Between here and the A265, the bridleway is a little overgrown in places, broad and easy in others. For much of the way it leads among trees. Ignore alternative paths, wander past Woodlands Farm, but when it forks in a wooded area just below a barn, take the left branch. This brings you past Lower Bough Farm (note the cowl on the oasthouse with its cutout shepherd, dogs and sheep) to the A265 on the edge of Burwash Weald. (Grid ref: 654235)

Turn right for a few paces, then cross the road to a drive leading to Burnt House Farm. At the end of the drive pass along the left-hand side of a converted oasthouse and into a meadow where there's a choice of paths. Continue directly ahead, but halfway along the field boundary cross a stile on the left and go down to the bottom corner of the next meadow. There you pass through a gate and follow the left-hand boundary of a large field to the far corner, then turn right and wander down a gentle slope (a woodland on the right). The way takes you into Bog Wood, but never strays far from the edge. Just before you leave it, go through a charming section where you gaze down onto the little River Dudwell meandering among trees. Out of the wood keep ahead on the bottom edge of a meadow for a short distance, before crossing a bridge over the Dudwell into the next field on the right. There you bear left, and on the far side of the field go through the right-hand of two gates. Follow a line of trees forming the left-hand boundary of the next field, but then veer left through a gap into the adjacent field, then bear right, soon rejoining the Dudwell. Through more trees soon have the Dudwell on the left and a feeder stream on the right. Ignore an alternative path going left, and keep ahead, soon with Bateman's seen ahead. The path follows the right-hand stream to a pond, goes round its left-hand side, passes a weatherboarded mill and comes to a drive. Bear left along this drive to Bateman's (2). (Grid ref: 671238)

Turn right on a narrow lane for about 200 yards, then cross a stile on the left and go up the right-hand edge of a field. At the top pass into the next field, go round the edge of a small woodland area and over another stile in the top boundary (lovely views behind). The path leads alongside hedges and through a meadow, then finally bears left where you rise up a last slope into Burwash, which you reach via the public car park behind The Bear Inn.

Items of interest:

1: Burwash is a typical one-time 'iron' village of the Sussex Weald, its houses and shops attractive with brick, tile or weatherboarding blending one against another in harmony on both sides of the High Street. The church of St Bartholomew at the eastern end of the village is part Norman, but much of it was sympathetically rebuilt in the mid 19th century. Nearby stands a war memorial where a lane runs south to the little River Dudwell, at which point a narrower lane breaks away to Bateman's. Contrary to the peaceful appearance of the village today, in the past Burwash was noted as being a place where "smuggling, sheep-stealing and burglary were rampant."

2: Bateman's was built for an ironmaster in 1634. An elegant stone mansion with lofty brick chimneys, it was discovered by Kipling in 1902 when he came down "an enlarged rabbit hole of a lane". It remained his home until his death in 1936. Among his writings during this period were *Puck of Pooks Hill* and his oft-quoted poem, *If*. Bateman's was bequeathed to the National Trust by Kipling's widow in 1939, and is open to the public during the summer months.

WALK 22
Herstmonceux - Herstmonceux Castle - Herstmonceux

Distance:	6 miles
Map:	OS Explorer 124 'Hastings & Bexhill' 1:25,000
Start:	The Woolpack Inn, Herstmonceux (Grid ref: 635126)
Access:	The village is on A271 about 5 miles north-east of Hailsham, and is served by bus from Hastings.
Parking:	Public car park at rear of The Woolpack Inn, access from West End. (Grid ref: 634126)
Refreshments:	Pubs, restaurant and shops in Herstmonceux, pub in Windmill Hill.

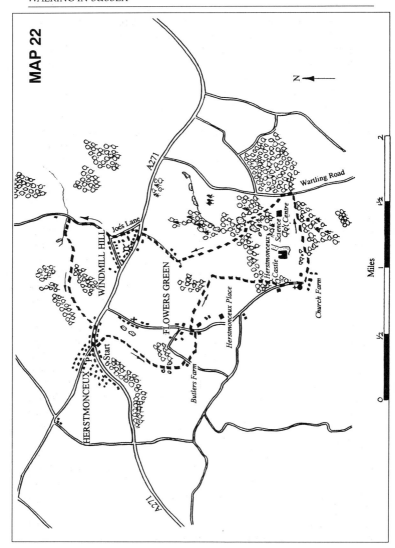

MAP 22

N

Miles

0   ½   1   ½   2

A271

Windmill Hill

Joe's Lane

Flowers Green

Herstmonceux

Start

Butlers Farm

Herstmonceux Place

Herstmonceux Castle

Science Centre

Wartling Road

Church Farm

A271

Gently undulating farmland provides long vistas across low-lying Horse Eye Level to the distant South Downs, giving a sense of spaciousness to much of this walk. But there are also enclosed sections through mixed woodland, and architectural features that both charm and confront the landscapes in which they are set. The tall-spired church at the southern limit of the walk is one that belongs to the countryside. The red brick elegance of Herstmonceux Castle adds a dimension of grandeur to a scene of tree-fringed pasture, while a set of ugly domed, silo-like buildings of the Herstmonceux Science Centre which formerly housed the Royal Greenwich Observatory, are painful blots on the landscape. Having said that, they add interest to the walk - and perhaps may inspire a return to visit them at leisure on another occasion.

*   *   *

Cross the main road in front of The Woolpack Inn to find the start of a tarmac footpath alongside a tile-hung cottage. This leads to the village hall and recreation ground, at the far end of which go through a kissing gate into a field and cross half-right, with the South Downs seen in the distance. Go through a second kissing gate by a barn, and walk directly ahead through a large field. On reaching the far boundary cross a stile and bear slightly left over the next field to another stile. Over this you'll see a pond just ahead with a track to its left. (Grid ref: 634117)

Go onto the track, bear right for a few paces, but before reaching a gate cut left across a narrow field to a gate in the right-hand hedge boundary. Passing through this make for a point about a third of the way along the left-hand boundary of the next field where you will find a plank footbridge over a ditch leading to another stile. Walk up the slope ahead and round the left-hand side of Butlers Farmhouse garden to come onto a narrow lane. Directly opposite the house cross a stile next to a field gate and wander up the left-hand edge of a sloping field. At the top corner cross another stile by a gate, then bear left through a field to its top left-hand corner. A house can be seen ahead. In the corner a stile gives access to a garden near a wooden barn. Pass the barn to your left and walk along the drive of Little Butlers to another narrow road in Flowers Green. (Grid ref: 637114)

Turn left, and about 20 yards later cross a stile on the right, then walk down the edge of a field, with several large greenhouses seen to the right, and the windmill from which the village of Windmill Hill gets its name, visible to the left. At the bottom of the field there are two stiles - one ahead, the other on the right. Cross the right-hand option and follow the bottom edge of a field to a gate by the corner of a wood. Pass to the right of the wood and up the slope beyond it, and at the top of the slope go through a gate then turn right in a hilltop field. Once more the South Downs can be seen ahead, the silo-like dome of the former Royal Greenwich Observatory (1) to the left, while to the right the large sanatorium-like building of Herstmonceux Place dominates the immediate scene. (It was apparently built of material left when Herstmonceux Castle was partially dismantled in 1777.) The boundary hedge leads down a slope to a junction of paths. Continue ahead on a track-like bridleway between fields, and soon after, when it veers slightly right, go ahead on a path leading to a wood. The path (the continuing bridleway) goes directly through the woodland and out to a country road. (Grid ref: 643104) Note the boundary stone on the right as you come to the road. It bears an anchor sign to indicate that the Observatory was originally administered by the Admiralty.

Turn left and soon pass between an entrance to Herstmonceux Castle (2) and the church of All Saints (3) - the latter being worthy of a visit. Just beyond the church the road gives way to a farm drive. Bear left and pass through a gate on a well-marked bridleway which leads for about $^3/_4$ mile to Wartling Road, and on the way takes you past the handsome frontage of Herstmonceux Castle and, on a wooded section, the green copper domes of Herstmonceux Science Centre. On gaining the road turn left, and a few paces beyond the entrance to the castle grounds, cross a stile on the left, walk through some trees and across an open meadow to its top right-hand corner. The Science Centre domes are seen close-by. Having reached the field corner the path enters a large mixed wood. In the middle of this come to a crossing bridleway and bear left, soon passing between a pair of reedy ponds. The path continues among trees until emerging at a gate to face a large field with three paths cutting through it. (Grid ref: 648110) Herstmonceux Place is once again seen half-left across the field.

Take the right-hand path which leads into a second field, maintains direction through the middle, and comes to Comphurst

Herstmonceux Castle

Lane. Turn right along the lane to the A271 in Windmill Hill, where you'll see The Horseshoe Inn nearby to the right. Cross the road, turn left and about 150 yards later, some way short of the windmill, bear right along a drive between houses (The Gables to the left). At the end of the drive a footpath continues between houses and comes to a small residential estate. Cross ahead and wander downhill to Joe's Lane. Bear left, and on coming to a junction continue ahead. Beyond a few houses the lane curves left, slopes downhill between high tree-topped banks, then bends right and left again. Immediately before the road crosses a stream go down a few steps on the left and into a field. (Grid ref: 651129)

Follow the stream, and when a footbridge takes you over another minor stream, bear half-left to a stile. Over this enter a narrow valley-like section and walk along its right-hand edge to find another stile in a corner. Crossing this walk ahead making for the right-hand edge of a strip of woodland where you go through a gap into a sloping field. A broad path/track takes you up the slope and into a second field. Maintain direction by a fence until reaching a hilltop field with houses on the far side. Keep alongside the left-hand boundary, but near the end veer half-right to a final stile above

127

an attractive house. Across this come to the A271 on the edge of Herstmonceux (4). Bear right and soon reach The Woolpack Inn.

Items of interest:

1: The Royal Greenwich Observatory was moved to Sussex in 1957 because of light- and atmospheric-pollution, but in 1979 the giant Isaac Newton telescope that had been housed in the large grey dome was transported to the Canary Islands. The Herstmonceux Science Centre now occupies a series of copper-domed buildings vacated by the RGO, and is open to the public from Easter to late October.

2: Herstmonceux Castle was built of rose-red brick in 1440 by Sir Roger Fiennes to defend the flat lands of Pevensey and Horse Eye Levels against potential invaders. Standing in a large moat in 550 acres of woodland and garden, it was one of the first sizeable buildings in England to have used brick since Roman times, but was partially dismantled in 1777. It has since been restored (in the 1930s) and the estate is now used as an International Study Centre in affiliation with Queens University of Canada. (The Castle grounds and garden are open to the public from Easter to November.)

3: All Saints' Church is Early English and full of interest. Perhaps the most notable features are the canopied Dacre memorial to the left of the altar, and the Fiennes brass on the floor of the chancel. The canopied memorial depicts Lord Dacre (died 1533) and his son, Sir Thomas Fiennes, although it has been suggested that the effigies may have been made for another family and brought here from Battle Abbey after the Dissolution. The Fiennes brass shows Sir William (father of Sir Roger who built the castle) in full armour. The brass is usually protected beneath a carpet.

4: Herstmonceux is noted as the birthplace of the Sussex trug - the wooden basket used by gardeners, still made in the village. Herstmonceux means 'the wooded hill of the Monceux family' after the Normans who came here in the 12th century and took on the manor. Architecturally, the village has a number of typical Wealden houses - a mixture of weatherboarded, tile-hung and old brick construction strung out astride a too-busy road.

South Stoke church dating from the 11th century dedicated to St Leonard, patron saint of prisoners. (Walks 30 & 31)

Arundel from the River Arun *(Walk 31)*
Looking across the Arun Gap *(Walk 31)*

WALK 23
Hailsham - Polegate - Hailsham

Distance:	7¹/₂ miles
Map:	OS Explorer 123 (16) 'South Downs Way Newhaven to Eastbourne' 1:25,000
Start:	Cuckoo Trail car park, Hailsham (Grid ref: 589094)
Access:	Hailsham stands astride the A295 southeast of the A22/A271 junction. Bus services from Eastbourne, Uckfield, Heathfield etc.
Parking:	Cuckoo Trail car park at northern end of Station Road, near The Victoria pub.
Refreshments:	Pubs and cafés in Hailsham, tearoom at Old Loom Mill, Mulbrooks Farm

The Cuckoo Trail is another of those linear recreational footpaths created along the route of a disbanded railway. This one makes a ten-mile journey across the Low Weald between Heathfield and Polegate, and the first 2¹/₂ miles of the following walk tackles the most southerly section almost as far as the Downs. It's a very popular route for both walkers and cyclists, surfaced with tarmac and with a number of sculptures (in both wood and metal) placed along the way. Once the outskirts of Polegate have been reached, however, our walk curves away to the east, then makes an arc round the edge of Pevensey Levels, crossing a series of fields and meadows drained by numerous water-courses, before rejoining the Cuckoo Trail for the final return to Hailsham.

*   *   *

Leave the Cuckoo Trail car park near The Victoria pub beside the A295, and turn right along Station Road. Before long you draw level with an attractive circular pond. Opposite this bear right into Lindfield Drive, then left into Freshfield Close, at the end of which you join the treelined tarmac path of the Cuckoo Trail proper. This is followed south for about 2¹/₂ miles, between fields for much of the way. On the walk you cross the B2104, and shortly after this, a very narrow lane. About 250 yards later pass the Old Loom Mill tearoom and craft centre on the left at Mulbrooks Farm. (Grid ref: 588073)

There are just two more minor country lanes to cross before you come to the edge of Polegate and a crossing path marked by an

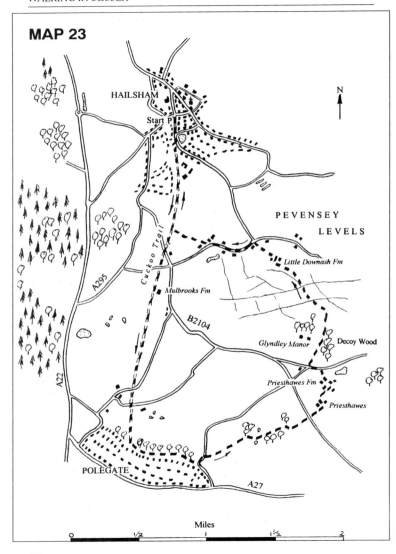

MAP 23

HAILSHAM

Start P

N

PEVENSEY

LEVELS

Little Downash Fm

Cuckoo Trail

A295

Mulbrooks Fm

B2104

Glyndley Manor   Decoy Wood

A22

Priesthawes Fm

Priesthawes

POLEGATE

A27

Miles

0   1/2   1   1 1/2   2

interesting metal sculpture. Turn left onto a good broad path among trees and follow this as far as Shepham Lane, from which point there's a fine view of the South Downs off to the right. Bear left along this very narrow lane until it makes a sharp left-hand bend. (Grid ref: 593052)

Go ahead over a stile and along the right-hand edge of a field. When the boundary cuts back to the right continue ahead towards the corner of a small woodland, then bear half-right to the top boundary. Go through a gap, then veer left to walk along the right-hand edge of another field marked by a woodland shaw. At the end of this bear right, then left, and soon come to the B2104. Maintain direction, now walking up the drive to Priesthawes. (Note the fancy wrought-iron gates, and pause to enjoy the view south to the Downs.) Remain on the drive as it curves just after a lodge, and pass the large house on your right. The drive bends sharply to the right and, unmade now, leads to farm buildings at Priesthawes Farm where it forks. Turn left and remain on the drive as far as Glynleigh Road. (Grid ref: 605064)

Turn left (lovely views to the Downs once more), and at a road junction soon after, cross two stiles on the right and walk ahead along the right-hand edge of a field. At the top corner another stile gives access to a junction of paths - only one of which is shown on the OS map. Bear half-left ahead and in a few paces go through a small wooded section, then over a plank footbridge into a meadow. After a few paces cross yet another stile next to a field gate, and bear half-right. There will now be a whole series of drainage ditches or water-courses to negotiate, each one with a simple plank footbridge. About 40 yards to the right of a small woodland go over a footbridge between meadows, and turn left. (An alternative path goes off to the right.) Come to a farm bridge spanning a broad stream unappetizingly known as Glynleigh Sewer, and once again bear left. In the corner cross wooden bars (no gate or stile here during research) and maintain direction. About 100 yards to the right of the field corner another stile leads into yet another meadow where you walk ahead over more meadows linked by stiles, making towards Little Downash Farm. Left of the farm cross a stile beside a gate and a pond, and walk towards the house. (Grid ref: 602076)

Bear left by the house and walk along the right-hand edge of a

Little Downash Farm, near Hailsham

small field with farm buildings on your left. Continue to a footbridge over the edge of a pond, and maintain direction to reach a road (Saltmarsh Lane) beside a house. Turn left and follow this road for about a third of a mile until it bends to the left. Leave the road and walk ahead in front of a barn/warehouse, and enter a field by a stile near a gate. Maintain direction along the right-hand edge of this, and two more narrow, fields, then rejoin the Cuckoo Trail. Turn right and retrace the outward route back to Hailsham (1).

Items of interest:

1: Hailsham was once noted as a 'string town' for its rope-making industry. In 1894 it was described as a "dreary little market town. The rope factory ... has the privilege of supplying the cords used in executions." Though the town may not have many obviously historic buildings, it is a pleasant enough place and not without its attractive features. To the east lie water-meadows, to the west the countryside is wooded, while the Downs rise in the not-so-distant south.

WALK 24
Buxted - High Hurstwood - Buxted

Distance:	7¹/₂ miles (or 7 miles route A option)
Map:	OS Explorer 135 (18) 'Ashdown Forest' 1:25,000
Start:	Buxted Station (Grid ref: 497234)
Access:	By train on the London Victoria-Oxted-Uckfield line.
Parking:	At the station
Refreshments:	Pubs in Buxted and High Hurstwood (route A option only)

Midway between Ashdown Forest and the South Downs, Buxted and High Hurstwood enjoy rural surroundings of considerable charm. Buxted has the gentle valley of the River Uck, tranquil lakes and a large, trim parkland. High Hurstwood is set among hills reached by a twist of narrow lanes, and is traversed by footpaths from which the very best of this folding land may be viewed. From sloping meadows far from the sound of roads, the distant Downs stretch as a line of blue upon the horizon; in the depths of leafy woods the busy chatter of birdsong is all that disturbs the silence.

*   *   *

Out of Buxted railway station bear left along the A272 for a few paces, then turn right by the Buxted Inn and walk along Framfield Road. Passing a number of houses the road slopes downhill and forks. Take the right branch. Curving left the road rises, and immediately before the entrance to Mascalls Farm you cut off to the right on a footpath which goes along the left-hand edge of a meadow, with the South Downs seen ahead. A squeeze stile on the far side leads into the next field by a small pond. The way progresses through a series of four fields in all, each linked by squeeze stiles. Across the fourth of these the path goes through a field gate and passes beneath the railway. (Grid ref: 495226)

Emerging from the tunnel a patch of scrub leads the way into a long meadow enclosed by hedges and trees. Wander through this to enter woodland at the far end, with a stream sidling through. A footbridge crosses a second stream, and a few paces beyond this you leave the trees to walk across a rough open meadow towards the white building of Buxted Park seen on the slope ahead. Pass between two lakes and bear left at a crossing path. The path comes

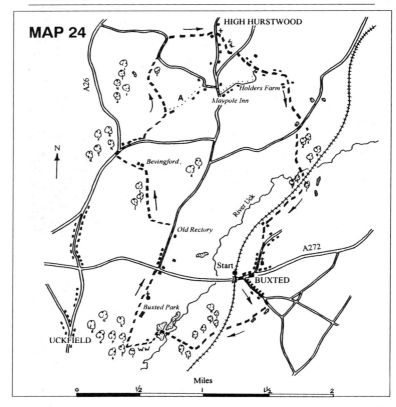

to a kissing gate, through which you join the Wealdway (1) and bear slightly right ahead. (Grid ref: 486225)

In a few paces come to a gateway and walk along the left-hand side of a fence. Soon reach a crossing grass path where you continue ahead to Views Wood, which you enter by a stile. Go down a short slope, then turn right immediately before a footbridge. Still following Wealdway signs walk up the slope when the path forks in a few paces and continue across parkland to a field gate and a stile. Here you enter the private estate of Buxted Park (2) and walk ahead

Buxted Park

alongside rhododendrons. Coming to the large house-turned hotel continue along the drive, soon passing the lovely church of St Margaret the Queen (3), which is well worth a visit. (Grid ref: 486230)

Remain on the drive that leads to the A272 by the wall surrounding Hogge House (4). Turn right, then left into Hurstwood Road by Buxted Primary School. Walking along this country road note Hogge Farmhouse on the left, followed by attractive cottages dated 1864. Remain on the road for about a third of a mile, then (100 yards beyond the entrance to The Old Rectory) go up some steps in the bank on the left and into a field by way of a stile. Walk along the right-hand edge of this field; again the South Downs may be seen in the distance to the left. About three quarters of the way along the field boundary cross a stile on the right, then go half left down the slope to a wooded corner where a footbridge spans a small stream and takes the path into another field. Go up the left-hand boundary, through a gateway and maintain direction through the next field alongside a wood, at the far end of which you come onto a drive by a farm (Bevingford). Follow the drive to its end at the A26. (Grid ref:

482249)

Bear right. In a few paces a minor road veers right signposted to High Hurstwood. Go down this for a short distance, and after passing a tile-hung house on the left the road curves right. Cross a stile on the left by a field gate and follow a track through an orchard. When the track ends continue ahead, now on a path that skirts the orchard boundary, descends a slope overlooking Stonehouse Cottage with a pond in its garden, then out through a gate onto a lane/driveway. Follow the lane for about 300 yards until a track forks left. Bear left with it, and in a few paces a path cuts off to the right. (Grid ref: 488255) This is the short-cut alternative walk, Route A, which should be taken if you are in need of refreshment, since it leads past The Maypole Inn.

Route A: Ascend a few steps into a narrow meadow and walk alongside a fence. At the far end cross a stile and maintain direction along the right-hand edge of another short meadow. A stile and more steps lead down into a sunken woodland shaw, through which the path can be rather muddy after rain. Out of the trees wander down a driveway passing a few houses until coming to a crossing lane. Bear right, and after a short distance come to a T junction and turn right again. The Maypole Inn is seen ahead, at the junction of two roads. Bear left at the pub and follow the lane past the Post Office Stores. After twisting its way for $1/2$ mile you come to a driveway on the left. This is where the main walk is rejoined at Grid ref: 499260.

Main Walk contd: Walk along the tree-lined track ignoring options to right and left until it leads into an open field. A short distance along the right-hand boundary brings you to a stile by a field gate. Over this maintain direction across a field divided by fences into paddocks. Go through these until a gate on the right puts you on a short track opening to a country road at a sharp bend. (Grid ref: 497262)

Walk ahead for about 300 yards, and when the road makes a sharp left-hand bend go to the right through a gap among trees, where a stile gives access to a sloping meadow. Go down the slope enjoying lovely views, then over another stile maintain direction to the foot of the slope where at the left-hand corner yet another stile takes you into woodland. Cross a footbridge and follow the path as it winds among trees and brings you onto a lane. Bear right for a few paces, then left towards the unusual turreted church of the Holy Trinity, High Hurstwood. Although there is nothing to indicate that you've done so, you have now joined the route of the Vanguard Way (5). Just before coming to the church go through a kissing gate on the right, and follow the right-hand edge of a meadow to a second kissing gate leading into a woodland shaw. The path takes you below a house, across a short patch of meadow and onto a country road. (Grid ref: 497263)

Bear left up the road, passing the drive entrance to Hadham House, and about 30 yards beyond turn right on a tree-lined path that leads to a track. Big views are glimpsed across the right-hand hedge. The track becomes a concrete farm drive by Royal Oak Farm, and at the end of the drive you come to a narrow lane near the entrance (on the left) to Hurstwood Farm. (Grid ref: 499260) Here the route is joined by **Route A** coming from The Maypole Inn.

Bear left along the lane, ignoring the drive to Hurstwood Farm. The lane becomes a stony drive, passes a few houses, then curves right. When it curves again to Holders Farm walk ahead on a footpath that goes between barns and a hedgerow. At the end of this hedge-lined section there's a junction of paths. Take that which continues directly ahead over a stile and down a short slope among trees, then on a footbridge into a field. Go slightly right across to the left-hand edge of a woodland where a stile takes you into a large field. Here you go half left to the far corner and onto a narrow road almost opposite the drive to Greenhurst. (Grid ref: 505253)

Turn right for a short distance, then over a stile by a field gate on the left where the road curves right. Cut across the field half right to find a stile in the lower corner by some trees. Heading through trees come into a large field and wander along its lower boundary beside a wood. After the wood ends a viaduct can be seen to the left ahead. At the end of the field cross a sturdy footbridge and continue through woodland, pass beneath the railway and into more trees heading slightly to the right, now leaving the route of the Vanguard Way. On emerging from the trees go round the right-hand edge of a sloping field to a stile on the far side. A fence-enclosed path leads on, parallel with the railway. Coming into another, final field, walk across it towards a barn. Just before coming to the barn cross a stile to its left, near a house, and go up a track beyond. This becomes a stony drive which in turn leads to a narrow lane, Church Road. Bear right and follow this past the church of St Mary the Virgin (6) and come to the main road in Buxted by the Buxted Stores. Turn right and wander downhill to the station.

Items of interest:

1: The Wealdway is a long-distance walk of 82 miles that leads from Gravesend on the Thames to Beachy Head near Eastbourne. See *The Wealdway & The Vanguard Way* by Kev Reynolds (Cicerone Press).

2: Buxted Park is a restored country house dating from 1725, built on the site of an earlier mansion. The architect, Basil Ionides, largely rebuilt the house following a fire in 1940. It is now a country hotel, health club and conference centre, set in splendid grounds that until the Great Storm of October 1987 had a fine avenue of lime trees. The grounds include lakes, woodland and mature rhododendrons. The original village of Buxted stood in the park, but in 1836 the then-owner of the house, Lord Liverpool, had the locals moved away to the present village site near the railway in order to give him more privacy; their cottages then being demolished.

3: The Church of St Margaret the Queen stands in the grounds of Buxted Park. Built in 1250, the unusual dedication is to Margaret, Queen of Scotland, and the splendid Jacobean pulpit, as well as the chancel ceiling, is decorated with marguerite daisies to further record the name. The plaster ceiling also has hop decoration, said to have been given by a former Rector in about 1600 as a thanksgiving for a rich hop harvest. There is much else to study here, including an ancient vestment chest, almost as old as the church itself, dating from about 1260, and in the churchyard outside a yew tree thought to be 2000 years old, some of its heavy old branches being held up by wooden props. The wall and ditch nearby is known as a ha-ha.

4: Hogge House, which stands at the entrance to Buxted Park, is named for Ralph Hogge, whose iron foundry is said to have made the cannons that led to the defeat of the Spanish Armada in 1588. The house was built in 1851, and it bears a cast-iron plate depicting a hog and the date. In the year of the Armada it was claimed that: "In this house lived ralf Hog who at the then furnace at Buxted cast the first cannon that was cast in England." Hogge became known as the father of the Wealden cannon-making industry.

5: The Vanguard Way, like its counterpart the Wealdway, links the suburbs with the sea. This 62 mile route begins at East Croydon, crosses the North Downs, Greensand Ridge, the Eden Valley and Ashdown Forest, then over High Weald ridges before coming to the South Downs and continuing to Newhaven via Seaford Head. See *The Wealdway & The Vanguard Way* by Kev Reynolds (Cicerone Press).

6: The Church of St Mary the Virgin is the Victorian church for present-day Buxted, built in 1885 by Father Wagner, a High Church priest, to serve the needs of villagers who had been relocated from their former homes in Buxted Park.

WALK 25
Isfield - Little Horsted - Isfield

Distance:	6½ miles
Map:	OS Explorer 123 (16) 'South Downs Way, Newhaven to Eastbourne' 1:25,000
Start:	Isfield Recreation Ground (Grid ref: 449174)
Access:	By road, Isfield is reached via Horsted Lane off A26, 1¼ miles south of junction with A22. The Recreation Ground is located along Station Road north of Isfield Station.
Parking:	At Isfield Recreation Ground (Grid ref: 449174)
Refreshments:	None on route, but pub in Isfield

Isfield lies quietly tucked away from the main road to Lewes, the River Ouse running along its western boundary, and the Uck sidling among farmland to the north. On this circular walk we follow the Uck upstream towards Little Horsted, then wander into a trim golf course laid out across a pleasant rumpled landscape, before returning to Isfield through more farmland. In the extravagent growth of midsummer, one or two sections of the route may be rather overgrown, although in winter and spring walking will no doubt be on easier paths.

*   *   *

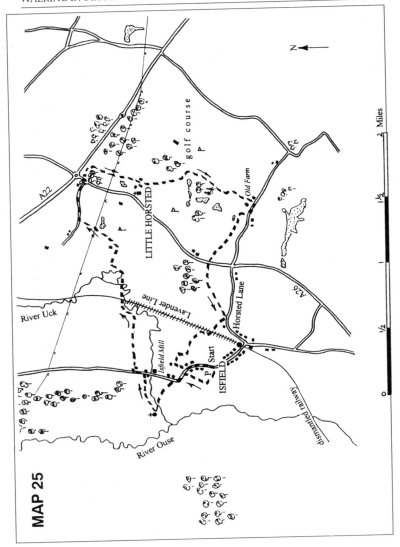

MAP 25

140

Begin on a hedge-lined farm drive which projects along the left-hand side of the Recreation Ground. When it begins to curve left after about 250 yards, turn right onto a footpath edging the right-hand boundary of a field (there is, in fact, direct access to this from the Recreation Ground itself). On the far side, about 40 yards from the corner, cross a stile onto Station Road and bear left. This soon curves to the right. Half-way round the bend a footpath cuts left between houses, and leads into another field, which you cross directly ahead. A gate on the far side gives onto a footbridge over the River Uck, and across this you continue ahead alongside a hedgerow to a second branch of the river. Now walk across to the church of St Margaret. (Grid ref: 444182) Unfortunately the church is kept locked, although the key may be obtained from a nearby cottage (details in the porch).

Bear right at the church and walk down the drive to where it joins Station Road opposite the Mill House. Bear left. (Note: a short distance to the right stands the tall building of Isfield Mill.) Soon pass the neat walled enclosure of Isfield Pound, and a few paces beyond the gateway of the first house on the right, cross a stile and walk ahead along the edge of a private garden. This leads to the side of a plantation, then through scrub into a field where you bear right. A stile in the far left-hand corner gives access to a broad grass track where again you head to the right. After passing through a farm gate maintain direction along the edge of a field, go over a stile in the top left-hand corner and continue ahead to the River Uck. (Grid ref: 456183)

Turn left. In a few paces the river makes an ox-bow curve, but we continue ahead to rejoin it soon after, over a stile beside a field gate. Follow the river upstream and before long pass beneath the skeletal remains of a bridge that once carried the Uckfield-Lewes railway. This marks the northern extent of the Lavender Line (1). The way continues directly ahead, passes along the right-hand side of a wood, and just beyond this crosses a stile and a plank footbridge to gain a farm drive. Bear left. This soon make a sharp bend to the right and comes to a golf course. When the drive curves left towards Keens Lodge, continue ahead on a stony track for another 40 yards, then cross a stile on the left and walk up the edge of a field to another stile on the far side. The path then veers right through a marshy patch of land, crosses another stile and a plank footbridge in a gap in a hedge, and re-emerges by the golf course again. Walk ahead to a drive, bear left and follow it uphill. When it curves left at the 11th green, leave it and go directly ahead. The way passes just to the right of an electricity pylon and reaches a narrow country lane. (Grid ref: 467189)

Bear right, and on reaching the A26 turn left. Halfway between the lane and the A22 roundabout, follow a bridleway off to the right. This leads alongside a woodland, at the end of which enter a large field on the right and walk along its right-hand edge. Coming to the brow of the field the South Downs can be seen ahead. So enter another golf course where a pond can be seen ahead to the right. Two tarmac paths can be seen nearby. Follow that which goes directly ahead, passing above and to the left of the pond. When this path curves to the right, walk directly ahead along the left-hand side of a row of trees and soon come to a field gate and a stile. Now walk along a drive between houses, and pass Little Horsted Primary School. (Grid ref: 472183)

A few paces beyond this come to a small parking area where the drive cuts sharply to the right. (Note: by taking this drive you can visit Little Horsted's church (2), a tranquil place in which to break your walk for a few minutes.) Walk through the car park and over a stile in the right-hand corner (this may be overgrown, in which case use the one in the left-hand fence and walk round to rejoin the correct path). Follow the hedgerow directly ahead, and just before this ends bear half-left to a tarmac path and a signpost. Cross the path ahead to a second path, pass below the right-hand end of a tee and continue on the edge of a woodland. At the end of this turn left on another tarmac path, and when it forks bear right. It soon forks again, and once more you take the right branch to cross a bridge over a stream. Signposting throughout this section of golf course is excellent. The way goes through the edge of Railands Wood, and beyond this bears left by a sign for the 12th green, and rises up a slope to a track junction. Turn right, soon leaving the golf course and coming to the outbuildings of Old Farm. Keep left of these and you will reach a country road. (Grid ref: 468170)

Bear right, and 100 yards beyond Old Farm go through a gate on the right, walk ahead alongside a hedge, then bear left. Passing above a pond come to a gap in a hedge, and walk ahead through two adjoining fields, so to reach the A26 to the left of some houses. (Grid ref: 462175) Cross with caution and pass through a gap in the opposite hedge. Maintain direction (views to the South Downs once more) to gain a corner of Wharton's Wood where you cross into a second field. Continue to a third field, across which you come to Horsted Lane. (Grid ref: 455174)

Do not go onto the lane, but instead walk along a track on the right which brings you into another field. On the far side cross a bridge over the Lavender Line, a short distance from Isfield Station. Now bear right along an enclosed footpath, and when this spills into a field through a kissing gate, continue ahead parallel with the railway, then cut left at the end of a fenced plantation. In the top corner of the field bear left into the next field and wander across towards a timber barn. Before reaching this, however, go through a gate on the right (about 50 yards from the end of the field) and ahead on a concrete farm drive. Just beyond some Dutch barns bear left on the continuing drive. When it veers left into a farmyard, leave the drive and go through a gate into the garden of a house. Keep along the left-hand edge, then bear left along the drive. This leads directly to Station Road, Isfield. (Grid ref: 449174) Turn left and walk back to the Recreation Ground car park.

Items of Interest:

1: The Lavender Line is the only section of track still open of the former British Railways Uckfield to Lewes line which closed in 1969. Now in the care of the Lavender Line Preservation Society, steam and diesel trains operate on Sundays and Bank Holidays throughout the year, Saturdays in June and July, and daily in August, with occasional 'specials' at other times. (Tel: 01825 750515)

2: St Michael and All Angels, Little Horsted is a pleasant, ageing church whose first recorded Rector is given as John, in 1230. The hamlet of Little Horsted consists of 60-70 houses in a parish of 2240 acres. Although it has no post office, pub or shop, there is a school with more than 100 pupils. This serves Isfield, Ringwood and Little Horsted. The large golf course through which the second half of the walk passes, belongs to the East Sussex National Golf Club, and covers land once owned by Worth Farm (mentioned in the Domesday

Book), and Hunningtons Farm whose records go back to the early 16th century.

WALK 26
Barcombe Mills - River Ouse - Barcombe Mills

Distance:	7¹/₂ miles (5³/₄ miles route A option, or 2³/₄ miles route B)
Map:	OS Explorer 122 (17) 'South Downs Way, Steyning to Newhaven' 1:25,000
Start:	Barcombe Mills car park (Grid ref: 434146)
Access:	By minor road ³/₄ mile west of Clayhill Nurseries on A26 north-east of Lewes.
Parking:	Public car park (unmade) 200 yards south-east of Pikes Bridge (Grid ref: 434146) - or at rear of Post Office in Barcombe Cross (Grid ref: 421157) and start walk there.
Refreshments:	The Anchor Inn on the River Ouse, pubs and shops in Barcombe Cross, pub and café near Barcombe Mills.

This delightful circular walk enjoys low-lying countryside with practically no hills to contend with - although the South Downs are never far away. The River Ouse dominates the first part. Where the walk begins the river forms several channels on which historic mills were once active. Upstream the remote, riverside Anchor Inn is popular on sunny lunchtimes, but elsewhere along the Ouse few buildings may be seen except an occasional farm nestling across the fields. Later the village of Barcombe Cross is visited, then Barcombe, site of the original village where the graceful church has the Downs as a backdrop. Two dismantled railways lie on our route, and at a former station on one of these, refreshments are to be had near the end of the walk.

*   *   *

Leave the car park at its western end (the far left as seen when entering from the road) on a footpath which leads to a driveway. Immediately before coming to a small hump-backed bridge, bear right through a squeeze stile, follow the path alongside a branch of the River Ouse (1), and cross a footbridge after a short distance. The continuing path goes through an open meadow, then between the river (on the left) and an embankment beyond which lies the unseen

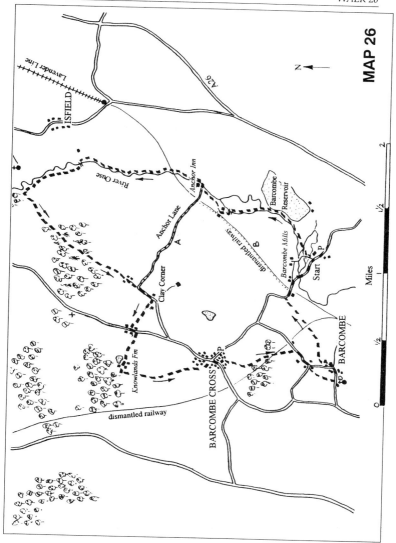

MAP 26

N

ISFIELD

Lavender Line

A26

River Ouse

Anchor Inn

Anchor Lane

A

Clay Corner

dismantled railway

B

Barcombe Mills

Barcombe Reservoir

Start

P

Miles

Knowlands Fm

×

BARCOMBE CROSS

P

BARCOMBE

P

dismantled railway

0   ½   1   ½   2

Barcombe Reservoir. On reaching a confluence of streams, both of which are branches of the same River Ouse, cross another footbridge in order to follow the left branch. Just before reaching some barns, go over a concrete farm bridge to the west bank again and bear right along a drive. When this curves towards a white weatherboarded house take the footpath ahead. (Grid ref: 439158) This curves behind the house and resumes alongside the river, and about 400 yards later brings you to The Anchor Inn. (Grid ref: 442160)

> **Route A:** If you bear left here and walk along Anchor Lane for almost a mile, at a point where the lane makes a sharp left-hand bend, you rejoin the Main Walk, thereby reducing the distance of this circuit by about 1³/₄ miles.

> **Route B:** A much shorter walk (2³/₄ miles in total) is possible by returning to Barcombe Mills from The Anchor Inn along the route of a dismantled railway, now accessible as a footpath. This is found a short distance to the west of the pub along Anchor Lane.

Main Walk contd: Recross to the east bank of the river and resume upstream. There are in fact two paths through the first meadow, but ours once again keeps company with the river. Pass beneath a bridge that once carried the railway between Uckfield and Lewes. (At Isfield, a short distance north-east of here, a mile-long stretch of this railway has been taken over by steam enthusiasts as the Lavender Line see Walk 25.) Beyond the bridge lies a very peaceful stretch of river, uninterrupted by roads or villages. On coming to a crossing farm track return to the west bank and a choice of paths. One gives an opportunity to return to Anchor Lane and Barcombe Mills, while ours bears right and continues upstream through three adjoining fields to a farm gate. Just before reaching this the spire of isolated Isfield church can be seen through trees ahead to the right. Go through the gate and turn left away from the River Ouse, now on a track. (Grid ref: 441181)

Heading between fields the track rises gently into a large mixed woodland, in which there are numerous crosstracks and pathways, but the one to take is always obvious. Just remain on the track (marked as Dallas Lane on the OS map) which leads all the way through, and eventually comes to a locked gate at the head of a short driveway, on either side of which stand lodge cottages. The gate is crossed with the aid of metal steps, and you walk ahead for about 100 yards where you join Anchor Lane at a sharp bend. This is where the walk is rejoined by **Route A**. (Grid ref: 429167)

Go straight ahead along the lane until it makes a sharp curve to the right at Clay Corner. On the left a drive breaks off to Banks Farm. On the right of the lane a stile gives access to a field. Pass to the right of a barn at Scobell's Farm, beyond which a second stile takes you into a narrow sloping meadow. Descend this half right, pass through a gap in the hedge and go up the right-hand edge of the next field. At the top right-hand corner a fine view of the South Downs may be had off to the left. Over another stile walk ahead along an enclosed path and come onto a country road by some houses. Turn left for about 40 yards, then enter a drive on the right to Knowlands Farm. This handsome house stands above a large pond, and you walk beyond the house and its various outbuildings, as far as a field gate on the edge of Knowlands Wood. (Grid ref: 419169)

Do not go through the gate, but turn left alongside the hedge with Barcombe Cross seen ahead, and the Downs beyond the village. On the far side of the field cross a stile and continue ahead, now on the left-hand side of a large field. In its top left-hand corner another stile takes you into a smaller field. Go over the Bevern Stream and along the edge of two fields to reach the village of Barcombe Cross. Walk ahead between houses, pass the village Primary School and a recreation ground, and come to the heart of the village at a three-way road junction. Turn right, soon to pass the Post Office (car parking at the rear). (Grid ref: 421157)

Turn left immediately before reaching The Royal Oak, walk along a narrow lane, and at a crossing road continue ahead along Mongers Lane. In a few paces bear right on an enclosed tarmac footpath leading to the corner of a field. Maintain direction along the right-hand boundary, and at its far side go over a stile onto a narrow grass terrace which once carried the East Grinstead-Lewes railway line (now served by the steam Bluebell Line between Kingscote and Sheffield Park). Go down the slope heading half-left on a path which goes under a power line and soon veers right through a kissing gate, then cuts through a strip of woodland. On emerging from the wood bear left round the edge of a field. At the field corner turn right and a few paces later, cross a stile on the left. Cut across to an oak tree in the right-hand boundary, and just beyond it you'll come to another stile. Over this bear half-left, and yet another stile will be found in the bottom hedgerow. This takes you onto a country lane, Church Road. (Grid ref: 422148)

Bear right. When the lane forks among some houses by a telephone box, bear right, and almost immediately enter the field on the left beside a white weatherboarded cottage. Walk ahead along the left-hand boundary, and at the bottom corner go through a kissing gate onto a lane opposite Barcombe church (2). This is approached along a drive which passes between a circular thatched round house, and a large pond seen across a hedge. (Grid ref: 418144)

From the church return to the lane and bear right. When it curves sharply left, turn right briefly onto the drive to Culver Farm. Pass through a gateway and turn left on a narrow drive, and when this curves right to Wychwood continue ahead on a hedge-enclosed footpath. On entering a field aim half-right across it, cross a ditch dividing this from the next field, and walk across it. On the far side a slightly raised embankment indicates once again the course of the dismantled East Grinstead-Lewes railway. Over this continue ahead through a series of interlinking fields and come onto a country road near a World War II pillbox. Bear right, and after 100 yards come to The Angler's Rest pub, which stands next door to the one-time Barcombe Mills Station (*refreshments*). (Grid ref: 429149) Continue along the road which shortly leads to the car park where the walk began.

Items of interest:

1: The River Ouse rises in the High Weald south of Crawley, and enters the English Channel at Newhaven. Barcombe Mills marks the upper extent of its tidal influence. In the Iron Age the river was used to transport charcoal for the Wealden iron industry, and it was first crossed at Barcombe by the Romans in the first century AD. Tolls were levied at Barcombe Mills in 1066, and a flour mill nearby was mentioned in the Domesday Book. In Domesday Barcombe was spelt Bercham, and was credited with having three and a half mills - the 'half' indicates that as it stood astride the stream dividing

The Anchor Inn on the River Ouse, near Barcombe Mills

the parishes of Bercham and Isfield. In Edwardian times Barcombe Mills was a fashionable picnic site. The last working mill here was built in 1870, but it ceased milling corn in 1934 and was destroyed by fire just five years later. The river has changed course many times, and in several places along the first stage of the walk various channels and field depressions indicate where previous windings have taken it.

2: Barcombe Church stands on the site of an earlier Saxon church. The present flint-walled building dates from the 11th century and is dedicated to St Mary the Virgin. The nave was built about 1100, the tower with its shingled broach spire was added in the 13th century. Inside the door on the right a charming engraved glass screen has as its theme, eternal life. Linked figures of women ascend heavenward. The original hamlet of Barcombe was decimated by the Plague in the 17th century, and the survivors moved away to build new homes in what is now Barcombe Cross. The barn and thatched round house nearby remain from the original hamlet. The tile-hung building by the pond in front of the church has been converted from two farmworkers' cottages.

WALK 27
Burgess Hill - Ditchling Common - Burgess Hill

Distance:	5¹/₂ miles
Map:	OS Explorer 122 (17) 'South Downs Way, Steyning to Newhaven' 1:25,000
Start:	Wivelsfield Railway Station (Grid ref: 321201)
Access:	By rail Wivelsfield and Burgess Hill Stations are on the London to Brighton line. Buses from Brighton, Hove and Lewes. Burgess Hill is on A273 north of Brighton.
Parking:	Free parking at Ditchling Common Country Park east of B2113/B2112 junction (Grid ref: 337180), in which case start the walk there.
Refreshments:	Pub and fish & chip shop near Wivelsfield Station, pub at Wivelsfield.

East of Burgess Hill a patchwork of field, meadow and woodland is criss-crossed by footpaths and bridleways. Modest hills of the Low Weald rumple the landscape, but to the south the Downs form a teasing wall. This circular walk laces that patchwork, visits a church set back from the village it serves, a pub whose landlord was murdered in the early 1700s, passes a Roman Catholic Convent, a few farms and a 15th century manor house. In addition there are ponds and a lake, woodland shaws and the heathland of Ditchling Common; a pleasant, undemanding walk, with lots of interest along the way.

*   *   *

Descend from Wivelsfield Station to a road by the railway bridge. With this on your immediate left cross the road, bear right and, passing shops, come to a junction by The Watermill Inn where you turn left. After about 250yds note a footpath sign on the right. The walk will return by this route later. For now continue ahead for a further 250yds to Theobalds Road (Grid ref: 323206), then bear right. Follow this road beyond Theobalds Farm, and when it makes a sharp left-hand bend cross a stile directly ahead and maintain direction alongside a hedge, then continue down a slope to a gap. Keep ahead in a second field, now with a hedge on the right. This leads to a stile over which you enter a woodland shaw, cross a footbridge, then up the right-hand side of the next field to skirt the

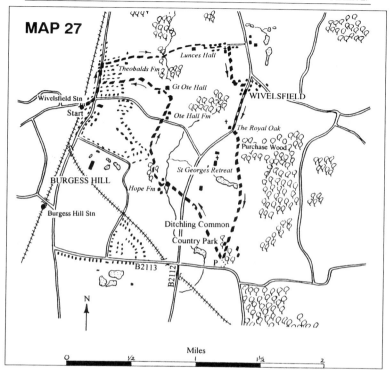

white building of Lunces Hall. Beyond this walk parallel with its drive, while to the right a fine long view shows the South Downs. Come onto the drive by a kissing gate and bear left. (Grid ref: 336208)

The drive leads to a few attractive houses and Wivelsfield Primary School, then the church of St Peter and St John the Baptist (1) which is worth a brief visit. Go down a narrow footpath (sign to Janes Lane) between houses and the churchyard wall. Enter a field and bear right, and at the end of the churchyard wall cut half left across the field to a stile and a choice of paths. Over the stile bear right to another stile in the boundary, and continue ahead across

151

this third field. On reaching the far boundary near a bungalow, go over yet another stile and a footbridge, walk ahead a short distance, then bear left to pass alongside the bungalow. Follow the drive until you come to the B2112. (Grid ref: 341202)

Turn right and walk along the road for 600yds until it bends by The Royal Oak (2). Cross the road to a bridleway in a copse. In a few paces this brings you to a path junction where you continue ahead, and leave the copse over a stile. Bear half-right to Purchase Wood and wander along its right-hand edge. A series of stiles now leads the path over a drive and into a parkland-like meadow well to the left of St George's Retreat (3). In the bottom left-hand corner go through a gate at the end of a lake, and maintain direction on a fenced grass track. Drawing level with a barn on the left, cross another track, go over a stile and wander through a field to the far boundary. Cross another stile and keep ahead, and at a crossing path continue between fences. The way leads to a drive, which you cross, descend steps into woodland and bear left. Within a few paces the path veers right to Ditchling Common (4) where you turn right on a crossing bridleway. (Grid ref: 338182) Here you meet the route coming from Ditchling Common car park.

Car Park route: At the right-hand end of the car park take a path heading to the right, parallel with the road. On coming to a T-junction of paths, bear left on a bridleway. Ignoring alternatives, this is soon joined by the Main Walk which enters from the right at Grid ref: 338182.

Follow the bridleway through gorse, trees and scrub along the eastern edge of Ditchling Common's open space. It takes you to the left of a solitary house, then the way forks. Veer left, still on a bridleway, and at a four-way crossing keep ahead to reach the B2112 road. (Grid ref: 334189)

Cross with care to a drive leading to Hope Farm. On the right-hand side go over a stile and walk down the meadow (sign to Hope Farm 1/4 mile) towards the farm. A footbridge takes you over a stream draining from a pond, then you come to the farm drive. Bear right, and a few paces later veer left ahead on a bridleway. Continue ahead when you arrive at a junction, but at the next bridleway junction soon after, veer left. This is on the edge of a residential area, and the bridleway goes between houses and fields. About 120yds after the second junction, take a footpath on the right into the corner of a field. The path cuts through this to a gate and a stile leading into a second field. Follow the right-hand boundary to another stile by a field gate. Over this again follow the right-hand boundary, so to reach a road. (Grid ref: 331198)

On the opposite side keep ahead along the drive to Ote Hall Farm. When it forks by the gates to Great Ote Hall bear left and remain on the drive until it makes a left-hand bend by some houses. Now go ahead along the right-hand edge of a field, enter the next field ahead and maintain direction to a third field. Once in this bear half-left. On the far side a fenced path leads between houses, crosses a residential street and comes to a road on the outskirts of Burgess Hill (5). (Grid ref: 323204)

Note: If you began the walk at the car park on Ditchling Common, turn right here. See the first paragraph for continuing directions from Theobalds Road.

Main Walk: Turn left, and on reaching the junction by The Watermill Inn bear right to Wivelsfield Station.

Items of interest:

1: Church of St Peter and St John the Baptist. Wivelsfield church stands within an attractive churchyard some way from the village. Note the carvings of an owl and a musician which flank the belfry window on the south side of the tower.

2: The Royal Oak at Wivelsfield was the scene of a murder in 1734, when a peddlar named Jacob Harris killed both the landlord and his wife. There is a memorial nearby.

3: St George's Retreat was formerly a Roman Catholic nunnery, begun in 1866 by Augustinian nuns from Belgium. The Retreat is now a Convent.

4: Ditchling Common covers an area of 188 acres and was established as a Country Park by East Sussex County Council in 1974. For centuries the area was part of a royal hunting ground, but now the Common provides open access to heath and woodland, and a small lake. Circular walks have been marked from the car park.

5: Burgess Hill has a tradition of brick- and tile-making, thanks to high-quality Wealden clay that is readily available. (This is not always appreciated by walkers!) Originally the area was noted for its agriculture, and for the annual sheep fair held on Fairplace Hill for more than 400 years. The coming of the London to Brighton railway in 1841 saw the start of its growth, and by the end of the 19th century Burgess Hill had become a thriving town boasting two stations (Burgess Hill and Wivelsfield). The name comes from the Burgey family who, in the late 13th century, owned a large farm near the site of the present railway station.

WALK 28
Henfield - Downs Link - Ashurst - Henfield

Distance:	8½ miles (6¾ miles route A, 7½ miles route B, or 7¾ miles route C option)
Map:	OS Explorer 122 (17) 'South Downs Way, Steyning to Newhaven' 1:25,000
Start:	Henfield High Street/Church Street junction. (Grid ref: 215162)
Access:	Bus from Brighton Old Steyne, Patcham etc. By car, Henfield is situated at junction of A2037/A281 about 9 miles north of Shoreham.
Parking:	Two public car parks in the centre of Henfield. (Grid refs: 216161 & 214161)
Refreshments:	Pubs, café and shops in Henfield, pub in Ashurst.

The Downs Link follows the route of a dismantled railway and, as its name suggests, serves as a link between the North and South Downs. Until Dr Beeching's axe severed this railway in the 1960s, Henfield had a station. But the loss of the railway is the walker's gain, and on this particular walk we follow the Downs Link heading south-west, with the South Downs making a gentle wall in the distance, then break away on the west bank of the River Adur, visit Ashurst and its lovely little church, and return to Henfield via another stretch of riverside footpath and the northern section of the Downs Link. As there are several alternative footpaths available, three optional 'short-cuts' are also given.

*   *   *

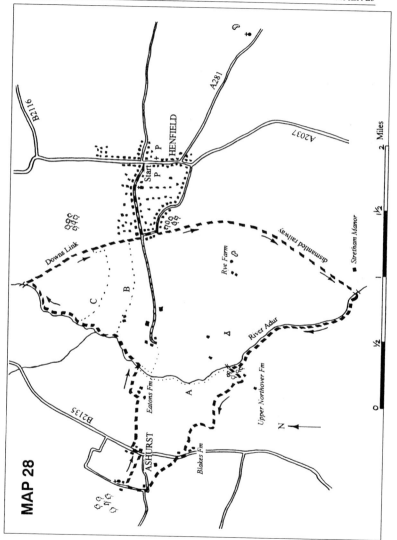

MAP 28

155

Leaving Henfield High Street walk down Church Street heading west. This becomes Upper Station Road, flanked by houses. A little over half a mile from the High Street you come to the Cat and Canary pub, and turn left into Station Road. When this curves sharply left opposite the Old Steam Mill, bear right, and a few paces later turn left onto the Downs Link footpath (1). At first blinkered by trees and bushes, this easy-to-follow path soon gains views of the South Downs ahead. Since it follows the course of an old railway there are no hills to contend with, for the way goes through shallow cuttings and along brief stretches of embankment, crossing minor streams and overlooking low-lying meadows of the Adur's valley. Just under two miles from the Cat and Canary, the Downs Link crosses the River Adur. (Grid ref: 200137)

Go through a gate on the right and wander upstream on the raised west bank. Gentle open countryside spreads on both sides of the river which is still tidal at this point, and the walk remains undemanding yet very pleasant. Here and there the way is interrupted by stiles or gates, but the footpath remains obvious. On reaching the small brick-built Northover Pumping Station an alternative path / track cuts off left, but we remain on the river bank for another half mile or so until coming to Bineham Bridge, a footbridge over the Adur. (Grid ref: 190152)

> **Route A:** Whilst the Main Walk makes a diversion across fields to Ashurst, an alternative option is to remain on the west bank riverside path for a further $^3/_4$ mile, to the next footbridge, where you rejoin the Main Walk described below at grid ref: 190162).

Main Walk contd: Immediately before the bridge turn left on a bridleway among trees. This is often very muddy for about 200 yards. Approximately 30 yards after joining the drive of a house, bear right through a gateway into a field. Cross this aiming half-right to locate a gate and a stile situated almost in the top right-hand corner. Over the stile enter a second field and walk alongside its left-hand boundary. At the top of the slope go through a gateway on the left, and again keep to the left-hand boundary. On reaching the top corner bear right, still within the field, and follow the hedge. When it cuts left through a gateway continue with it. The field narrows almost to the width of a track, and after passing through another gate you approach Blakes Farm. Go through the farmyard and out to the B2135 by Cedar Cottage. (Grid ref: 179156)

Turn right to walk along the road for a short distance. Rounding a bend cross a stile on the left into a narrow field aiming half-right to a footbridge and a second stile. Over this maintain direction to a third stile. Once again maintain direction, aiming towards the top corner of a larger field, well to the left of an imposing house. There you enter Ashurst Recreation Ground. Walk across to the far right-hand corner and a narrow road almost opposite Ashurst Primary School. (Grid ref: 175160)

Immediately past the school the road makes a very tight right-hand bend, then forks. Take the right-hand branch, Church Lane. Just before coming to a small stream note a footpath cutting off to the right. This is our route, but it is worth continuing along the lane for a very short distance to visit the tiny 12th century church of St James (2). Having done so, follow the path between the stream and a wooden fence, and when the fence ends continue ahead to rejoin the B2135 opposite The Fountain pub. (Grid ref: 180162)

Bear left along the road and soon draw level with the Village Hall. Just past this turn right and walk along a drive to Eatons Farm. Immediately before reaching this handsome farm bear left over a stile and walk ahead towards a pond. On reaching an oak tree in the middle of the field, turn right and in the right-hand corner cross a second stile. The path continues across two more fields and comes to the River Adur at a footbridge where the alternative **Route A** rejoins the walk. (Grid ref: 190162)

Cross the bridge and bear left, now walking upstream on the raised east bank. On coming to a gate and a stile an alternative return to Henfield is possible. (Grid ref: 193164)

Route B: Turn right on the path which cuts towards a neat thatched cottage. Passing Lashmars Hall and Blundens Farm the way continues heading roughly east (there are alternative options) and joins the path of the Downs Link a short distance from the Cat and Canary pub at Grid ref: 205162.

Main Walk contd: Remain on the river bank enjoying views north which includes the spire of the Carthusian monastery (3) near

Cowfold some three miles away. Come to the confluence of two arms of the river where, a few paces later, another path breaks away to the right. Ignore this and continue ahead to pass a small weir and a footbridge. Soon after this come to a gate where, once again, there's the possibility of an alternative return path to Henfield (4). (Grid ref: 195169)

> **Route C:** Take the right-hand path which soon crosses a stream by a footbridge, and continues alongside a second minor stream all the way to the Downs Link path and the Main Walk, which is rejoined at grid ref: 204167.

Main Walk contd: Following the Adur which has a few kinks in its course, come to Betley Bridge where you rejoin the Downs Link path. Turn right and wander back to Henfield along this route of the disused railway on a clear, firm path which comes to Upper Station Road by the Cat and Canary pub, being rejoined on the way by **Route C** and, by the pub, **Route B**. Turn left and retrace the outward route along Upper Station Road and Church Street to regain the High Street where the walk began.

Items of interest:

1: The Downs Link is an easy-to-follow recreational walking and riding route 33 miles long, which stretches from St Martha's Hill on the North Downs Way outside Guildford, to the hamlet of Botolphs where the River Adur breaches the South Downs near Steyning. The route follows the course of two defunct railways: the northern one from Guildford to Christ's Hospital near Itchingfield Junction; the southern which ran from Itchingfield Junction to Shoreham, both of which were closed by Dr Beeching in the mid-1960s. See *The South Downs Way & The Downs Link* by Kev Reynolds (Cicerone Press).

2: Ashurst Church, dedicated to St James, dates from the 12th century and is one of the secret gems of the district. At one time serving as a chapel for swineherds, it was built by the Knights Templar, and is walled with flint with a small spire rising from the tower. Apparently when it was being restored in 1877, the spire was left supported by oak beams while the tower was rebuilt below it. Unfortunately the door is often locked. In the village, The Fountain pub is thought to be at least 300 years old.

3: The Carthusian Monastery near Cowfold, whose elegant spire is seen from the banks of the Adur, is the only such monastery in the British Isles. Founded in 1873 when French Carthusians were facing persecution, the Victorian brick building of the Monastery of St Hugh's Charterhouse (as it is properly named), just to the south of Cowfold, houses thirty or so monks of this contemplative order behind high walls. The cells consist of what may be described as four-roomed cottages grouped around a cloister.

4: Henfield dates back to Saxon times when a small timber church was built in the 8th century. This was replaced in medieval times by one of Caen stone from Normandy, the stone having been shipped across the Channel and up the River Adur to the present site. The Victorians restored the church to such an extent that its character was drastically altered. Henfield became an important staging post on the London to Brighton coach road, and today it's a pleasant, bustling place on the edge of the Adur's water-meadows.

WALK 29
Pulborough - Wiggonholt - Pulborough

Distance:	3¼ miles
Map:	OS Explorer 121 'Arundel & Pulborough' 1:25,000
Start:	Barnhouse Lane, Pulborough (Grid ref: 053186)
Access:	Pulborough is served by train on the Horsham-Arundel line, and by bus from Midhurst. The village is on the A283 about 5 miles south-east of Petworth.
Parking:	Public car park on south side of the main road, behind The Oddfellows Arms (Grid ref: 053186)
Refreshments:	Pubs, restaurant and shops in Pulborough.

This short walk follows the River Arun, makes a horseshoe curve round Pulborough Brooks Nature Reserve, and visits a tiny out-of-the-way church. There's nothing strenuous about it, for there are no hills to contend with. Yet there are surprisngly long views to the South Downs wall, opportunities to study birdlife, and an option of extending the walk by obtaining a permit to explore the RSPB reserve and using their hides.

*   *   *

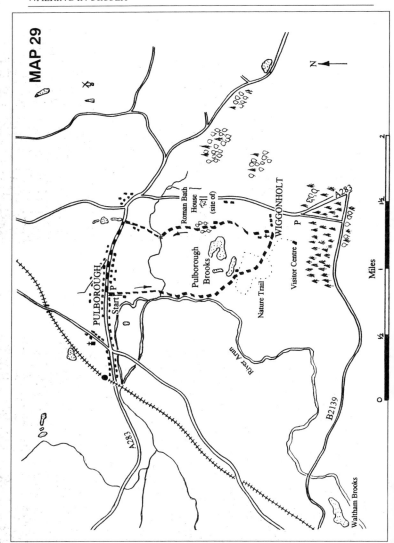

MAP 29

N

PULBOROUGH

Start P

Roman Bath
House
(site of)

Pulborough
Brooks

WIGGONHOLT

P

Visitor Centre

A283

Nature Trail

River Arun

B2139

Waltham Brooks

Miles

0   ½   1   ½   2

Bosham - home to sailors at high tide and
oystercatchers at low tide *(Walk 33)*
The Long Man of Wilmington *(Walk 35)*

The track to Glynde *(Walk 37)*
Home Brow, east of Ditchling Beacon *(Walk 38)*

From the centre of Pulborough (1) walk down Barnhouse Lane, a narrow drive which slopes down to a pretty cottage overlooking the former wetlands of the Arun Valley. (If starting at the car park, leave at the western end, descend steps to the lane and bear left.) At the end of the lane/drive cross a stile into a meadow and cross slightly left ahead. On the far side come to the River Arun and a footbridge over a feeder stream. Walk ahead on a raised embankment path following the river downstream. About 200 yards after going through a squeeze stile leave the river and bear half-left in Pulborough Brooks Nature Reserve (2). Initially this is a low-lying patch of grassland sliced with reed-fringed watercourses, and across it you go over a stile beside a field gate and veer left. Crossing a low slope come to an enclosed path with Little Hanger Hide to the left. (Grid ref: 055172)

Continue over the path (to right and left this is for permit holders only) and go through the centre of a large meadow to another gate and stile. Bear left and soon you'll cross another section of enclosed path (permit holders) with a little pond just beyond. Walk ahead towards Wiggonholt Farm and come to the tiny church of Wiggonholt (3) seen among trees on the left. (Grid ref: 060167)

Note: A path to the right of the drive leads to the Nature Reserve Visitor Centre for anyone who wishes to learn more about Pulborough Brooks, explore the 2-mile nature trail and/or make use of its four hides (entry fee for nature trail and hides).

Cross the drive by the entrance to The Old Rectory and enter a field which borders the grounds to the house. Walk along the left-hand edge, and maintain direction in a second field with large farm buildings seen ahead. At the left-hand corner come onto a track and walk ahead to a junction of tracks where you veer left on a footpath among trees and scrub. Once again Pulborough Brooks lie ahead, open stretches of water often busy with birdlife. The path takes you below and to the left of Banks Cottage, beyond which you will see two gates, one considerably higher than the other. Remain on the lower level and pass through the left-hand gate. (Hidden from here, the site of a former Roman Bathhouse lies off to the right.) The way continues above a minor watercourse and leads to a raised embankment with a footbridge crossing a tributary of the Arun. (Grid ref: 060180)

Over the bridge veer right, and follow the field edge to a stile in the top right-hand corner. The path continues between trees and bushes, comes to a drive and this in turn leads to the main A283. Turn left and wander back to Pulborough.

Items of interest:

1: Pulborough overlooks the River Arun and the water-meadows of Amberley Wild Brooks. The Romans crossed the Arun here when building their road from Chichester to London, and a staging post was provided for travellers using it. West of the village Stopham Bridge, built in 1423, is considered by many to be the finest medieval bridge in Sussex.

2: Pulborough Brooks Nature Reserve attracts large numbers of ducks, geese, wading birds and swans, while in summer nightingales, dragonflies and butterflies feature. The reserve is owned by the RSPB who maintain four hides and a 2-mile nature trail. The Visitor Centre is housed in the converted Upperton Barn (entrance by road via the A283 about 2 miles south-east of Pulborough), and includes a tearoom and information area. (RSPB Pulborough Brooks Nature Reserve, Wiggonholt, Pulborough RH20 2EL - Tel: 01798 875851)

3: Wiggonholt Church has no patron saint, and was apparently built for the use of shepherds working the Brooks. It is one of the so-called 'Wild Brooks Churches' which include those of Amberley, North Stoke, Parham and Greatham - the parish has been linked with that of Greatham since 1508. The original walls of the church date from the 12th or 13th century, and the font is late-Norman. There's a list of Rectors and Curates which goes back to 1422, while baptism records are from 1510.

WALK 30
Amberley - South Stoke - Amberley

Distance:	6¹/₂ miles
Map:	OS Explorer 121 'Arundel & Pulborough' 1:25,000
Start:	Amberley Railway Station (Grid ref: 026118)
Access:	By train on the Horsham-Arundel railway line. By road via B2139 about 4¹/₂ miles south-west of Storrington.
Parking:	With consideration in Amberley village - in which case start the walk by Amberley church. (Grid ref: 027133)
Refreshments:	Pub in Amberley, café and pub a little west of Amberley Station.

On this gentle outing we visit one of the loveliest of all Sussex villages and one of the most remote of its churches, follow the River Arun as it threads a way through the South Downs, and look upon a series of exquisite landscapes. This is a walk to gladden the heart of any photographer, and every true lover of the countryside.

*　　*　　*

Out of the station go to the main road (B2139) and bear right past the entrance to Amberley Industrial Museum (1). Follow the road as it gradually rises, and shortly after the footpath ends, bear right into High Titten Lane. This is bordered by hedges, but as you progress along it so there's a huge panoramic view to the left. Near the head of the slope turn left in front of a large house (Highdown). Almost at once there's a charming view ahead to Amberley Castle and church. The lane leads down to the B2139 which you cross directly ahead and walk into Amberley (2). In the heart of the village turn left to the church. (Grid ref: 027133)

With the church to your left continue on the road below the soaring curtain wall of the castle, and then go ahead on a footpath between trees. Cross the railway line and wander through low-lying meadows with the spire of Bury church (3) ahead. Unfortunately there is no bridge across the River Arun here, so we cannot visit Bury on this occasion. Instead, bear left on a raised grass embankment and follow the Arun (4) downstream for about ³/₄ mile as far as a grey steel footbridge. (Grid ref: 022121)

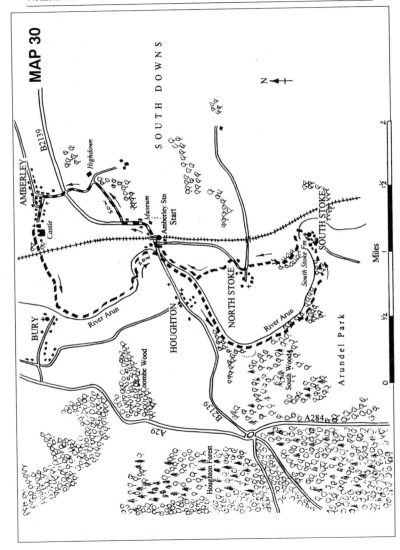

Cross to the south bank and continue downstream, now along the right bank whose footpath leads to Houghton Bridge and the B2139 again. (This is only a very short distance from Amberley Station.) Should you need refreshments at this stage of the walk, bear left across the bridge where there's a riverside café on the left, and a pub on the right. For the continuing walk cross the road and resume along the river bank, soon passing below the village of Houghton. In places the path squeezes among trees and scrub close to the river, also in patches of woodland and below one-time chalk pits whose exposed cliffs tower above the trees. In a while you come to a flintstone wall surrounding Arundel Park and follow this in a long wooded strip. The path eventually emerges from the trees to an open field where you continue ahead along the left-hand edge. At the bottom corner the way goes through another woodland, then comes out to another field. Remain in the field and pass to the right of a barn, and on coming into a yard in front of North Stoke Farm, take the upper of two tracks on the right. In a few paces you will come to a narrow lane. (Grid ref: 026099)

Bear left and follow the lane past a few houses, then on a track to the left of South Stoke church (5) - worth visiting. The track leads to another bridge across the River Arun. Over this bear left and about 150 yards later turn right onto a raised footpath cutting through a woodland area. Shortly after crossing a neat wooden suspension bridge leave the trees and walk along the left-hand edge of a field, at the top of which you cross a track and continue to a narrow lane in North Stoke. (Grid ref: 023118)

Bear left, then right along the lane (Stoke Road), and about 20 yards beyond a house on the right, go through a gate on the left to follow a footpath among scrub leading once more to the Arun. Bear right and follow the river upstream to Houghton Bridge and the B2139 yet again. Turn right to Amberley Station.

Items of interest:

1: Amberley Industrial Museum was created from an extensive chalk quarry which at one time employed over 100 men. The 36 acre site has a variety of industrial machines on display, as well as a narrow gauge railway. It is open between May and October Weds-Sundays, and daily throughout the summer school holiday period.

(Tel: 01798 831370)

2: Amberley has many attractive cottages of assorted styles and materials, a number of which are thatched and whose gardens burst with colour that cascades over walls above the road. There's a pub (The Black Horse) and a village store, and next to the Norman church the ruins of a castle built for the Bishops of Chichester in 1380 around an existing manor house, and used as a summer residence by the bishops until the 16th century. The castle is now a hotel and restaurant. St Michael's church, possibly built by Bishop Luffa (who also built Chichester Cathedral) in 1100, has an elaborately carved archway leading to the chancel, while to the right of it can be seen the faded survivors of wall paintings thought to be about 800 years old. Virginia Woolf wrote of Amberley as "an astonishing, forgotten, lovely place between water meadows and downs". E.V. Lucas described it as "sheer Sussex". Few would disagree with that.

3: Bury church, dedicated to St John the Evangelist, contains a 14th century rood screen, while its tall shingled spire can be seen far across the water-meadows of Amberley Wild Brooks. Bury village has a secluded air, but it used to be linked with Amberley by a ferry across the Arun. Victorian novelist, John Galsworthy, lived in the mock-Tudor Bury House from 1926 until his death in 1933.

4: The River Arun is the longest in Sussex, rising in St Leonard's Forest near Crawley and cutting through the South Downs between Amberley and Arundel before finding the sea at Littlehampton. The river is popular with anglers for whom chub, pike, perch and roach are likely to be caught. The Arun Valley was one of the six 'rapes' (administrative divisions) into which the Normans divided Sussex following the 1066 Conquest. Each rape contained a strip of Wealden forest for hunting, an area of farmland for cultivation, downland for grazing, and an all-important coastal strip.

5: South Stoke Church is dedicated to St Leonard, patron of prisoners, and was built in the 11th century. It occupies a very secluded and peaceful site; indeed the only means of access by motor vehicle is via the narrow dead-end lane which starts by Arundel Castle. The church is a simple, unfussed place, with flint walls and a curious spire like a dunce's hat. When I visited bees were swarming from a nest over the porch, house-martins were darting to and fro with food for their young, and three black-faced rams grazed among the gravestones as the churchyard maintenance team.

WALK 31
Arundel - South Stoke - Burpham - Arundel

Distance:	8 miles (also via route A option)
Map:	OS Explorer 121 'Arundel & Pulborough' 1:25,000
Start:	Arundel High Street/Mill Road junction (Grid ref: 019070)
Access:	By train on the Horsham-Arundel-Littlehampton line
Parking:	Several public car parks in Arundel, or car park in Burpham behind George & Dragon pub (Grid ref: 039089), in which case start the walk there.
Refreshments:	Pubs & cafés in Arundel, pub in Burpham.

There's a world of difference between the tourist-busy streets of Arundel and the remote seclusion of South Stoke church, and on this outing we not only experience those contrasts, but also the high and wide expanse of the Downs, shaded woodlands, the delights of the River Arun, and the dignified beauty of Burpham - a village with much to reward a visit. The Arun is a major feature, and it dominates the second half of the walk, while from the heart of Arundel Park, a high point on the crest of the Downs forming the western 'gatepost' of the Arun Gap, a most impressive view of the Arun Valley is gained, gazing north to the flat emptiness of Amberley Wild Brooks where a glint of sun on water reveals the river's distant meanderings. Below, on opposite banks, both South Stoke and Burpham have churches that are worth spending time in, and the latter village also has some very attractive cottages with a 'back-of-beyond' air of tranquillity to them. This is a walk that rewards a leisurely approach. Choose a day of bright promise, pack some sandwiches, a camera and, maybe, a pair of binoculars, and let the hours drift by.

Note that much of the first half of the walk goes through Arundel Park - dogs are not allowed - which is closed to the public on 24 March each year.

*   *   *

At the bottom of the High Street in Arundel (1), by the bridge over the River Arun, Mill Road cuts off to the north. The walk begins by

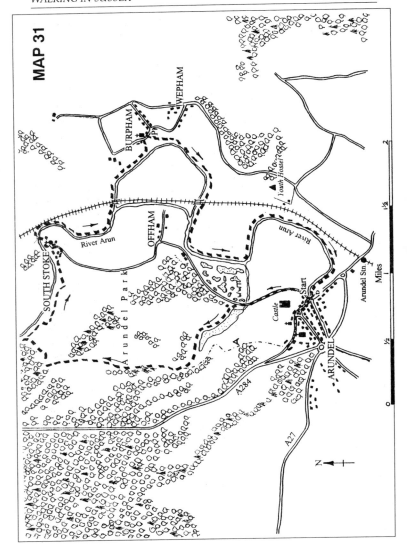

heading along this road, although an alternative start is given below, as Route A.

Route A: This option misses the popular beauty spot of Swanbourne Lake, but sees more of Arundel town. Walk up the High Street to the top of the hill, and when the castle wall breaks back to the right, follow a footpath which soon enters Arundel Park, goes through woodland, passes to the right of the flint- and stone-built Hiorne Tower, then slopes gently down into a narrow, steep-walled valley. There you join the Main Walk at grid ref: 012086.

Main Walk contd: Passing the gatehouse entrance to Arundel Castle wander along the road until you come to Swanbourne Lake on the left. Continue on the road to a gate at the north side of the lake. Arundel Wildfowl Reserve (2) is ahead to the right. Through the gate on the left (refreshments at Swanbourne Lodge) follow the path alongside the lake, and when you come to the far end, continue directly ahead into a narrow coombe, or valley. This curves to the right and then forks. At this point the path of **Route A** joins ours from the left. (Grid ref: 012086)

Walk ahead up a narrow path which climbs a steep slope dividing the two branches of the valley, just to the right of a fence-enclosed woodland. Near the head of the slope go over a stile and continue across a large open downland - a big panorama unfolds as you make progress, especially behind to the distant sea. Ahead stretches a long blanket of woodland, and the path makes for the left-hand end, crosses a stile and shortly after comes onto a track. Wander ahead with the wood to your right, but when the track veers leftwards away from it, maintain direction and, in a few paces, gain a wonderful expansive view across the Arun Valley. (Grid ref: 013098) In that view there are patchwork field systems on the Downs, chalk cliffs on both sides of the river, the villages of Houghton and North Stoke, Bury church and Amberley Castle, the Houghton bridge over the Arun, and the river itself winding sedately through the low-lying meadows.

Go down the slope a little to a stile next to a field gate. Over this follow a chalk track downhill, and near the foot of the slope among trees bear right at a crossing track. Emerging from the trees South Stoke church can be seen ahead. On coming to a gateway turn left away from the track and walk down the edge of South Wood - farms at North Stoke seen across the valley directly ahead. In woodland come to the flint wall which surrounds Arundel Park and follow this leftwards for a short distance until a tall kissing gate takes the path through. Bear right on a woodland path just above the river, which takes you past a number of straggly box trees. After a while the trail rises to an open field. Maintain direction along the left-hand side and re-enter woods at the bottom corner. The path comes out again on the approach to South Stoke Farm. Keep in the field to pass above a large grey barn, and on coming to a yard in front of the farm, turn right alongside a brick-built barn to reach a narrow lane. Bear left and follow the lane as it curves in front of some houses, then veers right as a track on the left-hand side of South Stoke churchyard (3). (Grid ref: 026100)

Beyond St Leonard's church cross the Arun on a farm bridge and turn right onto the raised riverbank path. Rounding a bend in the river ignore an alternative path which breaks off left and continue along the raised path, soon gaining a fine view across to the church and few houses of South Stoke which you've just left. When the river curves again, Burpham can be seen ahead. The river divides and the path crosses a railway line. Continue alongside the river, passing below Peppering Farm, then cross a stile next to a field gate and walk ahead slightly right as a track goes uphill. Over another stile beside a second field gate resume alongside the river, now with a view to Arundel Castle far ahead to the right, and Burpham church near at hand to the left. The path briefly deserts the river, climbs among scrub and trees and then forks. Bear left to wander up into Burpham (4). (Grid ref: 039089)

Turn right at the top of the slope and, with the church on your left (worth a visit), turn right in front of The George & Dragon. Walk across the recreation ground along its left-hand side, with the pretty hamlet of Wepham seen to the left. At a junction of paths continue directly ahead and soon descend steps to another path junction. Maintain direction, now on the river bank again, and once more with Arundel Castle ahead. Shortly before coming to the railway line another path cuts left and is the one to take if you plan to stay overnight at the youth hostel. Otherwise remain on the riverbank. Over the railway line chalk cliffs can be seen above the Black Rabbit pub at Offham. The two arms of the Arun come together, then it curves again in front of the pub. Across the river the ponds and lakes of the Wildlife Reserve are shielded from view by tall reeds. Remain on the riverside path all the way back to Mill Road in Arundel where the walk began.

Items of interest:

1: Arundel is an attractive and extremely popular small town with a number of good 18th century houses as well as the Norfolk Arms, a one-time coaching inn in the High Street. The town is dominated by the Castle. Originally built shortly after the Norman Conquest by Roger Montgomery, Earl of Shrewsbury, in order to defend the valley from sea-borne raiders, it was almost destroyed by the Parliamentarians in 1643, rebuilt in the 18th century and restored in 1890. Since the reign of Richard III it has been in the possession of the Dukes of Norfolk. Opposite the castle, across the top of the High Street, stands the elegant Catholic Cathedral of Our Lady and St Philip Howard. Although it has the appearance of a 14th century French Gothic cathedral it was, in fact, built only in the 1870s.

2: Arundel Wildfowl Reserve is run by The Wildfowl & Wetland Trust (WWT) which was founded by Sir Peter Scott at Slimbridge in Gloucestershire in 1946. WWT Arundel has 60 acres of lakes, ponds and reedbeds, and more than 1,000 ducks, swans and geese. There's a Visitor Centre as well as seven hides, a restaurant and tea room. The Reserve is open daily throughout the year except Christmas Day. (Tel: 01903 883355)

3: South Stoke Church dates from the 11th century and is worth visiting. Although simple and, by comparison with many other places of worship in the area, quite bare, there is a beauty in its simplicity. At the back of the church a local poet has contributed three type-written books of poems that resonate with the ambience of the area. There's also a board adorned with a variety of notes of local historic interest.

4: Burpham is an attractive small village of scattered flint and brick cottages, some graced with thatch, reached by a 3-mile dead-end lane. The name comes from *Burg* meaning 'fort', and *ham* meaning village, and was first mentioned in the 10th century as Burghal Hidage. In the time of raiding parties of Danes, Alfred the Great decreed that five forts should be built between Lewes and Chichester. One of these was at Burpham, earthworks of which can clearly be seen today south of the recreation ground. Excavations in the 1970s uncovered several Saxon buildings inside. The church was mentioned in the Domesday Book, and it is suggested that a pagan shrine existed on the site before the Saxon building was raised. Although the present church of St Mary the Virgin is built almost entirely of flint, Roman tiles appear in its fabric, while the most striking feature is the beautifully carved 12th century arch. South of the church is The George & Dragon inn which dates from 1736.

WALK 32
West Stoke - Kingley Vale - Stoughton - West Stoke

Distance:	6³/₄ miles
Map:	OS Explorer 120 'Chichester, South Harting & Selsey' 1:25,000
Start:	West Stoke Car Park (Grid ref: 825088)
Access:	By minor road 2 miles west of A286 at Lavant, north of Chichester.
Parking:	The car park is located west of West Stoke House.
Refreshments:	Pub in Stoughton

A fairly strenuous, but very rewarding walk, this offering crosses an arm of the South Downs from a hamlet of cottages and farms to a secluded village with a Saxon church and a popular pub. The ascent of the Downs is made by way of Kingley Vale Nature Reserve, noted for its wonderful old yew trees, while the summit is marked by a row of ancient burial mounds and an extensive panorama, including a focus of Chichester Cathedral to the south-east, and the sea beyond that. Choose a day of settled weather and allow plenty of time to explore the Nature Reserve and to take in the magical views from the walk's high point.

*   *   *

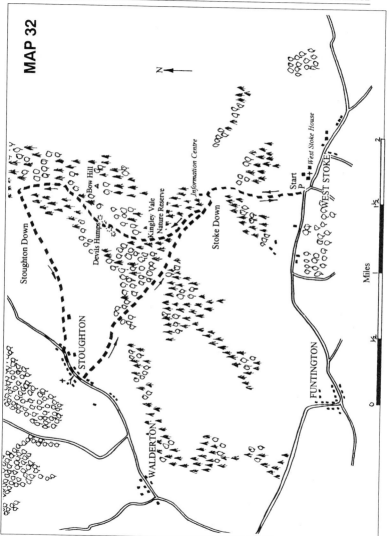

MAP 32

Stoughton Down

Bow Hill

Devils Humps

STOUGHTON

Kingley Vale
Nature Reserve

Information Centre

Stoke Down

WALDERTON

FUNTINGTON

Start
P

West Stoke House

WEST STOKE

Miles

N

The walk begins at the western end of the car park where a footpath sign indicates the way to Kingley Vale, giving 20 minutes. A pleasant stony path heads north between fields with the wooded slopes of the South Downs ahead. Coming to a woodland area the path forks, the two branches reuniting soon after. When you come to a crossing path at the entrance to Kingley Vale National Nature Reserve (1), note a wooden sculpture just ahead. Beyond that, secluded among trees, is an unmanned information building, or field museum (recommended). (Grid ref: 825099)

Bear left and when the bridleway forks shortly after, turn right on a more narrow chalk path which rises along the edge of the Nature Reserve. As you gain height, note another trail climbing parallel to the right. When an opportunity arises, cross to this path and follow it uphill. The way veers slightly right, enters woods and makes height through a charming grove of yew trees that clothe the steep slope, before emerging on the crest of the Downs by a row of burial mounds known as the Devil's Humps (2). Views to the right show Chichester and the sea, while ahead beyond the tumuli you gaze across the shallow valley of the little River Emms to other downland ridges fading blue with distance. Go between the humps onto a crossing bridleway and veer right to pass to the left of Bow Hill's summit. (Grid ref: 824113)

The bridleway is soon flanked by woodland, but eventually the left-hand side opens to grassland on Stoughton Down. On the far side of this open area come to a massed junction of tracks and bear left on a path which edges another woodland section and brings you to a seat from which you overlook the Emms Valley. Wander downhill on the route of the Monarch's Way (3). The path becomes a farm track, and at the foot of the slope feeds onto a narrow road on the outskirts of Stoughton. Note the handsome house (Bartons) on the right. Bear left into the village. Soon after passing The Hare and Hounds a minor road cuts away to the right to the Saxon church of St Mary, which dates from about 1050. About 150 yards beyond this turning, bear left onto a concrete drive by the side of Tythe Barn House. (Grid ref: 801114)

This becomes a track rising again to the Downs and passing on the way a memorial to a 23 year-old Polish pilot serving in the RAF, who died in November 1940 when his Hurricane crashed in the field on the left following aerial combat with a German ME 109. The angle steepens after this and enters woodland. The trees give way just below the downland crest. Ignore alternative paths and continue ahead alongside more woodland, with views to the sea ahead and to the right. The path slopes downhill and enters woods, once more of yew and beech, and before long rejoins the upward route near Yew Tree Grove. Follow the now familiar route back to West Stoke car park.

Items of interest:

1: Kingley Vale National Nature Reserve is noted for its magnificent yew forest, the largest in Britain. Yew trees flourish on downland slopes, but some of those at Kingley Vale are thought to be among the oldest living plants in the country. In the bottom of the valley behind the field museum (but not on our route) the finest and strangest of these trees are to be found. Some gnarled old specimens create arches, tunnels and caves, their branches bending to the ground where they take root and reappear as neighbouring trees. The forest fans out and spreads up the slope towards the ridge,

allowing only spokes of light through on the brightest of days. The Nature Reserve was established in 1954, and is designated a Special Area of Conservation. It is rich in wildlife, with fallow deer, 33 species of breeding butterfly, and 57 species of breeding bird. The sculpture at the Reserve entrance is entitled *The Spirit of Kingley Vale* and was carved by Walter Bailey from a single piece of yew from a tree destroyed by the Great Storm of October 1987.

2: The Devil's Humps on Bow Hill are prehistoric burial mounds dating from the Bronze Age (2000-800 BC). They

'The Spirit of Kingley Vale'.

were plundered by treasure seekers in the 19th century. The Tansley Stone nearby was placed as a memorial to the first chairman of the Nature Conservancy Council, Arthur Tansley, who was directly involved in establishing the Nature Reserve in 1954.

3: The Monarch's Way stretches for 609 miles and is based on the escape route of Charles II following his defeat at the Battle of Worcester in 1651. It starts in Worcester, and after passing through no less than 11 counties, ends at Shoreham. A 3-volume guide to the route has been produced by Trevor Antill (Meridian Books).

WALK 33
Bosham - Fishbourne - Bosham

Distance:	4 miles (or 5¾ miles route A option)
Map:	OS Explorer 120 'Chichester, South Harting & Selsey' 1:25,000
Start:	Bosham Church (Grid ref: 804038)
Access:	Turn south off A259 3 miles west of Chichester. Nearest station - Bosham (1¼ miles). The village is also served by bus from Chichester.
Parking:	Public car park (pay & display) east of the church. (Grid ref: 805039)
Refreshments:	Pubs & cafés in Bosham and Fishbourne.

An easy, level, farmland walk, this heads east from the picturesque sailing centre of Bosham to the edge of Fishbourne. The first village has links with King Canute and Harold Godwin (later King Harold), while Fishbourne has one of the largest Roman sites in Britain. The longer version of the walk also explores a short stretch of Fishbourne Creek which, in common with Bosham Channel, forms one of the arms of Chichester Harbour. And for much of the outward route, the spire of Chichester Cathedral is a powerful reminder of the glories of that small city just a short distance away.

* * *

Bosham Church looks west to the water, while the lane which runs along the south side of the churchyard is backed by attractive houses. With your back to the water walk along the lane towards the village (1), and when it forks by The Anchor Bleu take the right-

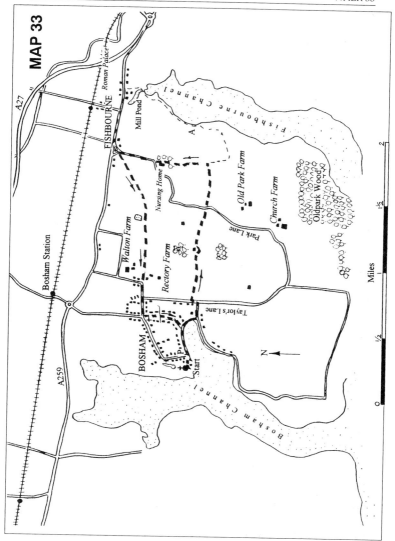

MAP 33

FISHBOURNE

Roman Palace

A27

Mill Pond

Fishbourne Channel

Bosham Station

Walton Farm

Nursing Home

Old Park Farm

Church Farm

Park Lane

Oldpark Wood

A259

Rectory Farm

Taylor's Lane

BOSHAM

Start

N

Bosham Channel

Miles

177

hand option - unless it is high tide, in which case pass to the left side of the pub. The low tide option leads to Bosham Quay where you turn left along a road (this is flooded at high tide). The high tide alternative comes to a crossing road where you walk ahead along a tarmac footpath, at first between houses, then opening just above the road followed by the low tide route. Whether you are on the footpath or the road continue to the head of the creek from which you have a pleasant view back to the village. Passing alongside a white-walled bungalow, note that this was once the local school. At a T-junction of roads turn left, and at the next T-junction go left again along Taylor's Lane. (Grid ref: 812036)

About 50 yards later bear right onto a footpath. On crossing a small watercourse turn right, then left over a second footbridge onto a track. This is flat, low-lying country, with the South Downs seen far off to the left. The track ends at a cottage, but a footpath goes round the right-hand side and continues along the left-hand edge of a field. At the top corner go through a gap where the path is confined between a windbreak of trees and a fence leading to Park Lane. Maintain direction through the middle of a large open field with Chichester Cathedral enticing ahead. Continue on the left-hand edge of a second field, on the far side of which you come to a junction of paths. (Grid ref: 829037) The main route heads to the left, while the alternative, right-hand, path is for those who wish to see Fishbourne Channel and the opportunity to visit the Roman Palace.

Route A: Turn right, then left at a watercourse, where the footpath continues to the edge of Fishbourne Channel. Wander along the sea wall as far as a millpond, then turn left into Fishbourne (2). The remains of the Roman Palace are on the north side of the A259 and are clearly signed. For the continuing walk turn left along the main road (*refreshments*), and on the outskirts of the village bear left into Old Park Lane. At the next junction rejoin the Main Walk (Grid ref: 830047) by going directly ahead along a footpath/farm track.

Main Walk contd: Turn left at the path junction along the edge of another large, flat field. In the left-hand corner walk ahead between two open fields, then on a track among trees as far as a narrow lane by the entrance to Beggar's Roost Nursing Home. Continue along the lane until it forks. (Grid ref: 830047) This is where **Route A** rejoins our walk.

Turn sharply to the left on a path / farm track alongside a line of windbreak trees. Ignore a second track cutting left and go ahead to a T-junction of tracks. Take the footpath ahead which passes below and to the left of a farm reservoir hidden behind a grass embankment. The path eventually brings you onto a country road by the entrance to Rectory Farm, with a lovely thatched cottage to the right. Ignoring alternatives wander ahead until coming to The Berkeley Arms. Immediately before a telephone box turn left onto a tarmac path which is led between houses, across a residential street and on to a second residential street which goes straight ahead. A short way down this bear right into Harbour Road which leads to the head of the creek with Bosham Quay seen a short distance away.

Items of interest:

1: Bosham seems to have been taken over by the sailing fraternity, with both arms of its channel lively with yachts when the tide is in. When it's out slender ribbons of water ease through mudflats where gulls and oystercatchers pace, wheel and cry. Along Bosham Quay high tides flood the road and leave it strewn with seaweed. Several cottages are thatched with almost unreal perfection; others are flint-walled or built of faded, mellow brick. Holy Trinity church, separated from the water by an open greensward, is depicted in the Bayeux Tapestry. It has a Saxon tower and a justly famous chancel arch; it also has Roman foundations and Roman bricks in the walls. The grave of a child is said to be that of Canute's daughter, and tradition has it that it was here that the Saxon king failed to turn back the incoming tide. Three decades after Canute, in 1064, Harold Godwin, later King Harold, entered Bosham Church to pray before sailing for Normandy. There he swore to help William capture the English crown, and it was the breaking of this oath that led to the Norman invasion two years later.

2: Fishbourne would probably be unremarked as nothing more than a suburb of Chichester had not a workman digging a trench in 1960 unearthed some Roman tiles. His find led to eight years of concentrated excavation which revealed the site of a Roman palace built about AD75. The north wing is now enclosed in a protective hangar, its wonderful mosaic floors containing a panel some 17ft square displaying a winged boy astride a dolphin. Other remains on show include sections of wall, baths and a heating system, as well as formal gardens - all suggesting that the palace had been built for an important dignitary, possibly Cogidubnus, the Roman viceroy.

WALK 34
Exceat - East Dean - Seven Sisters - Exceat

Distance:	8 miles
Map:	OS Explorer 123 (16) 'South Downs Way, Newhaven to Eastbourne' 1:25,000
Start:	Seven Sisters Country Park Visitor Centre (Grid ref: 519995)
Access:	On the A259 reached by Eastbourne-Seaford bus. Exceat is also served by the Ramblerbus from Berwick Station via Alfriston. This service operates on summer weekends and Bank Holidays.
Parking:	Public car parks opposite and behind the Visitor Centre.
Refreshments:	Pub and restaurants in East Dean, café at Birling Gap, and at the Visitor Centre.

This walk offers a variety of interests. The two small villages of West and East Dean are full of attractive buildings. The churches at Westdean, East Dean and Friston are all worth visiting. Then there's Friston Forest and the surprise view of the sea from a short signposted diversion, a glimpse of Friston Place through whose parkland the walk progresses, and the downland of Went Hill overlooking the huge arc of the sea. And of course there's the helter-skelter walk across the Seven Sisters, the breach in the cliffs at Cuckmere Haven, and the inland return to Exceat alongside the Cuckmere itself. A walk with pleasures all the way.

*   *   *

Where the minor road from Litlington joins the main Seaford-Eastbourne road a few paces west of the Living World and Visitor Centre, a footpath, signposted to Westdean, goes into woods and passes through a car park before entering Friston Forest proper.

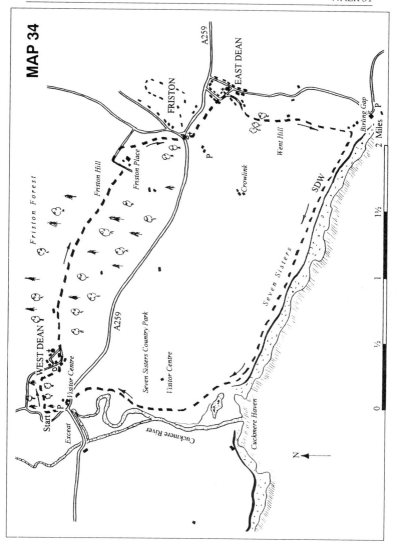

MAP 34

FRISTON

EAST DEAN

A259

Friston Forest

Friston Hill

Friston Place

P

Crowlink

Went Hill

Birling Gap

P

SDW

2 Miles

1½

WEST DEAN

Visitor Centre

Start

P

Exceat

Seven Sisters Country Park

Visitor Centre

Seven Sisters

1

½

0

Cuckmere River

Cuckmere Haven

N

Although there are several alternative trails stay with the main path as far as Westdean (1), which you reach by a duck pond. Turn left briefly in front of Pond Cottage, then right along a narrow road (sign to Friston 2 miles). The road curves round a flint wall, rises uphill and forks. Our route continues ahead, uphill, but it is worth making a short diversion left to visit the lovely 12th century Parish Church of All Saints - note too the 13th century Rectory next door.

Continuing uphill the Forestry Commission road takes you directly up to the main part of Friston Forest (2) where a stony track continues ahead, signposted to Jevington and Friston. After passing a house on the left the track forks. Follow a broad bare-earth path striking uphill, the left-hand option being the route to Jevington, and soon the way becomes another stony track. Wandering easily through the forest note the sign off left to a viewpoint. This is gained by a short diversion which provides a surprise view across the roof of the forest to the sea. The track slopes downhill and curves left, Leave it here and continue ahead on a minor track. At the foot of the slope come to a crossing track and maintain direction on a grass path which leads to the open pasture of Friston Hill. From here the way descends to a narrow lane by the entrance to Friston Place. (Grid ref: 546988)

Turn left along the lane which soon veers sharply to the right, while a track continues ahead. Stay on the lane and about 250 yards later cut off to the right on an unmarked footpath which goes through a gate and across open parkland. On the far side a kissing gate in a flintstone wall gives access to the drive leading to Friston Place. Over the drive enter another section of parkland which you cross to the far upper corner. There a stile takes the path through another wooded area to where a minor road from Jevington joins the main A259. (Grid ref: 552983)

Cross the main road to a pond, then enter the churchyard of St Mary the Virgin, Friston (3). Walk through the churchyard and out to a view of the sea. The way now leads down through a lovely sloping meadow to East Dean (4), which you enter by the village hall. Bear right along a street, soon passing the village green on the left, beside which stands The Tiger Inn. The street forks. Take the upper, right-hand branch and when this ends go through a field gate into a meadow and curve slightly leftwards, rising along the

The Seven Sisters

lower edge of more woodland. The path then makes a steady climb through a section of woodland and emerges onto the open downland of Went Hill.

The path over Went Hill slopes down to Birling Gap (5), but unless you need refreshments it is not necessary to go quite as far as that. Instead, a few paces after passing through a gate by a white weatherboarded cottage, bear right through another gate on the path which takes you across the Seven Sisters. This is part of the South Downs Way. Crossing the Seven Sisters is a glorious breezy walk with fine views all the way. The steep dry valleys between the hills are known as 'Bottoms', while most of the hills, or Sisters, are named 'Brow' - Flagstaff Brow, Rough Brow, Short Brow etc. The final hilltop is Haven Brow, named for the view it affords of Cuckmere Haven. Continue down the slope, cross a stile then veer right, descending gently to the grassy levels of the Cuckmere basin. There you wander along a good path which leads all the way back to Exceat and the Seven Sisters Country Park Visitor Centre (6).

Items of interest:

1: Westdean is a charming, unspoilt hamlet nestling in a downland bay and almost completely surrounded by Friston Forest. In Saxon times King Alfred had an estate here (he had another at Steyning), but there is no sign of the palace he is said to have built in AD850, although the site may lie beneath the ruins of a medieval manor house in the heart of the village. During Alfred's reign, the Cuckmere estuary was much more extensive than it is today, and it is thought that he maintained a fleet here. (It was then known simply as Dene.) The 12th century Parish Church of All Saints is well worth a visit. The tower has an unusual half-hipped spire, and among the memorials is one to Sir John Anderson (Churchill's wartime Home Secretary) whose name was given to the air-raid shelter. Note the flint-built 13th century Rectory next door, the two making a very pretty picture. (There is another West Dean north of Chichester in West Sussex.)

2: Friston Forest is owned by South East Water, but managed by the Forestry Commission. It consists of almost 2000 acres of mixed woodland, with broad rides and footpaths cutting through, including one arm of the South Downs Way and the Vanguard Way. Originally the forest was almost entirely deciduous, and during the 15th century it sheltered remnants of Jack Cade's peasant army.

3: Friston has now spread to the point of almost swamping nearby East Dean. The little church of St Mary the Virgin stands on the western edge of the village, on the opposite side of the A259, and has a small window above the south doorway reckoned to be early Norman. Friston Place, seen on the approach to the village, dates from 1650.

4: East Dean (not to be confused with East Dean in West Sussex) is also sometimes spelt as Eastdean. The Tiger Inn, which dates from Elizabethan times, is one of the oldest of its buildings. While the village has virtually merged with Friston to the north, there was also a scheme for further development to spill into the lovely Crowlink Valley, but campaigners (among them, Rudyard Kipling) fought to preserve it, and it is now in the care of the National Trust.

5: Birling Gap is where the eastern end of the Seven Sisters dips into a dry valley. Once frequented by smugglers, this part of the coast was notorious for shipwrecks, and in the 18th century the Rev. Jonathan Darby, vicar of East Dean, had a tunnel cut through the chalk cliffs which opened to a cave overlooking the sea. On wild nights of storm, Darby lit a fire there as a warning to passing mariners. Today the buildings which huddle at the Gap are in danger of falling into the sea as the clifftop is eroded by the waves.

6: Seven Sisters Country Park was established by East Sussex County Council in 1971, but is managed by the Sussex Downs Conservation Board, who also manage the neighbouring Seaford Head Nature Reserve. Covering 690 acres of land spreading east of Cuckmere Haven, it is heavily used by walkers, for whom the walk across the Seven Sisters to (or from) Birling Gap is a noted classic. The Visitor Centre is housed in a converted 18th century barn.

WALK 35
Alfriston - Wilmington - Jevington - Alfriston

Distance:	9 miles (or 8¹/₂ miles route A option)
Map:	OS Explorer 123 (16) 'South Downs Way, Newhaven to Eastbourne' 1:25,000
Start:	Alfriston Parish Church (Grid ref: 522030)
Access:	By bus from Seaford. A Ramblerbus also operates a summer service (weekends and Bank Holidays) from Berwick Station through the Cuckmere Valley. Nearest railway stations at Berwick and Seaford.
Parking:	Public car park at northern end of Alfriston village (Grid ref: 521053)
Refreshments:	Pubs and restaurants in Alfriston; the Eight Bells pub and tearooms in Jevington.

Extensive downland views are just one feature of this lovely circular walk. There are several churches, two villages (apart from Alfriston), a 1600 year-old tree, close examination of the famed Long Man of Wilmington, and in summer-time at least, paths lined with wild flowers. From Alfriston the walk begins alongside the Cuckmere River, then breaks away across low-lying fields to Wilmington. After pausing to absorb the delights of this fine village, the way continues towards Wilmington's noted chalk figure,

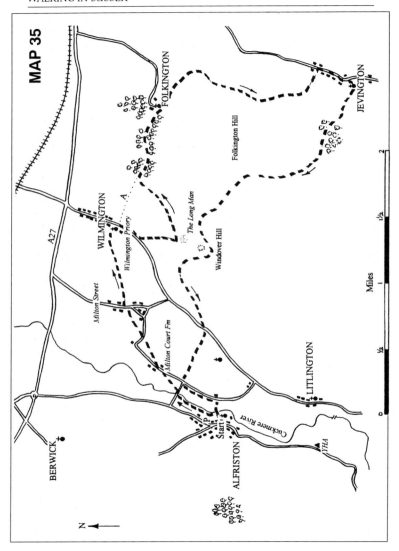

MAP 35

BERWICK

A27

WILMINGTON

Wilmington Priory

A

FOLKINGTON

Folkington Hill

JEVINGTON

The Long Man

Windover Hill

Milton Street

Milton Court Fm

LITLINGTON

Start

P

Cuckmere River

ALFRISTON

YHA

N

Miles

0   ½   1   ½   2

makes a traverse of the downland slope at mid-height in order to reach Folkington church, before cutting round the flank of Folkington Hill to Jevington. The return to Alfriston is achieved by climbing up to Windover Hill above the Long Man's head (with a magnificent panorama), followed by a gentle descent to the Cuckmere once more. All in all, this is a glorious walk.

*   *   *

From the church, go down to the Cuckmere, bear left and follow the river upstream until you come to a brick-built road bridge (Long Bridge). Cross to the east side, and go through a kissing gate on the left where a footpath cuts through two fields. A second kissing gate then gives onto a minor road. Once again bear left, and about 200 yards later, opposite Milton Court, cross a stile on the right into a field corner. In a few paces go into the adjacent field where a footpath cuts directly ahead, crosses the road and continues to a stile located to the right of a Dutch barn. At a path junction in the next field, maintain direction towards the right-hand end of farm buildings, and once again come onto the minor road in Milton Street. (Grid ref: 535041)

Bear left for about 100 yards, then turn onto a track on the right, opposite Milton Street Farm. Wandering between large open fields, the spire of Wilmington church is seen ahead. At the head of the slope the Long Man of Wilmington (1) comes into view. The track leads directly to Wilmington churchyard, and you walk through this to the village street, passing between the church of St Mary & St Peter (2) (Grid ref: 544043) and a huge, ancient yew tree (3).

Route A: This slightly shorter option does not go to the Long Man, but climbs the hill-slope opposite the church. On emerging from the churchyard cross directly ahead onto a signed bridleway. This is eventually joined by the Main Walk at the start of a woodland section, marked as The Holt on the map. (Grid ref: 551040)

Main Walk contd: Bear right along the road to pass Wilmington Priory (4), then take the footpath on the left which at first parallels the road, before veering left towards the Long Man. Just below the chalk figure go through a gate. Here the path divides. Take the left branch, which is less obvious than the other. This skirts the lower slope of the Downs with huge views across the Low Weald, while off to the left the continuing escarpment of the South Downs fades into the distance. The way rises gently, and at a junction of paths goes through another gate on the edge of woodland to join the direct bridleway of route **option A** at what is known as The Holt. (Grid ref: 551040)

The walk continues among trees for about ³/₄ mile, and follows a section of the Wealdway (5), eventually coming to a track by St Peter's Church, Folkington (6).

Veer slightly right to pass the church on your left, on a stony track which, some way beyond the church, narrows to a footpath. Avoid alternative paths to right and left and keep to this main route for about a mile, tracing the lower edge of Folkington Hill - at first heading south-east, then curving more to the south and south-west. In summer the hedge-lined path is adorned with wild flowers. Shortly before reaching Jevington come to a crossing track and bear left. (Grid ref: 561021)

The main road in Jevington (7) is reached opposite the Old Post Office. Here you turn right and soon come to The Eight Bells pub. (The Wealdway continues its journey to Beachy Head opposite the pub.) Walk a little further along the road, and when the path rises above it, follow this into Jevington churchyard through a swivel gate. Go through the churchyard to a small car park, and bear right on a footpath which forms part of the South Downs Way (8). (Grid ref: 561015)

At first fence-lined at the end of a series of paddocks, the path then rises through woodland and comes to a junction of trails. Continue ahead to a broad path (an extension of the track which was joined shortly before reaching Jevington). Maintain direction, and emerging from the woods near the head of the slope at another junction, bear right. Soon a view opens off to the right to the Pevensey Levels as the path leads onto the open Downs. The way eventually curves left round the head of a deep coombe (Deep Dene) and passes through a gate. Bear left and wander along the side of Windover Hill, whose summit is the site of a long barrow. (Magnificent views from the hilltop, which is just above the head of the Long Man.) Beyond the summit the path curves right then left, and slopes down to a narrow lane. (Grid ref: 532033)

Continue on a footpath opposite, and when this spills out at a junction of lanes cross half-left ahead, go through a gate into a field and turn left. The Cuckmere flows through this field, and the spire of Alfriston church is seen ahead. On the far side of the field come to a crossing path just below a converted barn (Great Meadow Barn - formerly known as Plonk Barn and shown as such on the OS map - was built in 1698 and restored in 1985). Turn right, cross the Cuckmere River and enter Alfriston.

Items of interest:

1: The Long Man of Wilmington is a giant outline of a figure cut into the chalk of the Downs below Windover Hill, facing north. In each hand the figure holds a staff about 250 feet long, and he can be seen from a considerable distance. Although his origin is unknown, he was traditionally thought to have been created in the Bronze Age, about 4000 years ago. Others speculate that he was carved by Saxons. But whoever was responsible for this, the most famous of all chalk figures in Sussex, they cleverly designed him in such a way that he is never seriously foreshortened from wherever he is viewed, despite the steepness of the hill.

2: The church of St Mary & St Peter was founded in the 11th century, about the same time as the Priory next door, but it has been much restored.

3: The Yew Tree beside Wilmington church is thought to be about 1600 years old. It is huge, its ancient limbs supported by timber props and chains.

4: Wilmington Priory was founded soon after the Norman invasion by Robert de Mortain, the Conqueror's half-brother, and was dissolved 400 years later by Henry VIII. It is now open to the public by the Sussex Archaeological Society. In the wall surrounding it is the village pound, formerly used for holding stray animals.

5: The Wealdway is a fine, 82-mile long-distance route which links the Thames with the English Channel, beginning at Gravesend in Kent and finishing on Beachy Head outside Eastbourne. See *The Wealdway & The Vanguard Way* by Kev Reynolds (Cicerone Press).

6: St Peter's Church, Folkington dates from the 13th century. Like so many others along the Downs it has a squat shingle spire projecting from a flint-walled tower. Inside there are box pews and among the memorials, one to Viscount Monckton who was an advisor to Edward VIII during the days leading to the abdication.

7: Jevington is said to be the one-time haunt of smugglers who came inland from Birling Gap. The main village street has some attractive flint-walled houses and a popular pub (The Eight Bells), once owned by smuggler, James Pettit, known as 'Jevington Jigg' who was eventually sentenced to serve 17 years in Botany Bay. The church of St Andrew's, tucked away in a side lane, has a Saxon tower thought to have been built about AD900-950. The north wall of the nave contains a Saxon sculpture of Christ defeating the dragon of Evil with a cross-shaped sword. One of the means of financing the church's restoration in Victorian times was by the sale of its bells - as the following verse records:

> *Jevington folk are very proud people,*
> *They sold their bells to mend their steeple*
> *And before they are left in the lurch,*
> *They would sell the steeple to mend the church.*

8: The South Downs Way was officially opened in July 1972 and is the only National Trail that is both a footpath and bridleway. It has two starting places in Eastbourne, and ends 102 miles later in Winchester. See *The South Downs Way & The Downs Link* by Kev Reynolds (Cicerone Press).

WALK 36
Alfriston - Bostal Hill - Alfriston

Distance:	7³⁄₄ miles
Map:	OS Explorer 123 (16) 'South Downs Way, Newhaven to Eastbourne' 1:25,000
Start:	Alfriston Parish Church (Grid ref: 522030)
Access:	By bus from Seaford. A Ramblerbus operates through the Cuckmere Valley from Berwick Station at weekends and Bank Holidays in summer. Nearest railway stations at Berwick and Seaford.

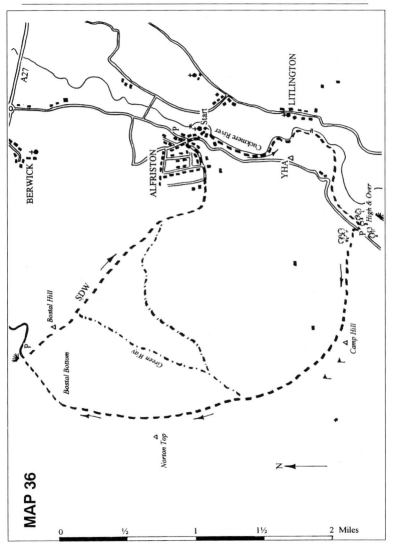

MAP 36

BERWICK

LITLINGTON

ALFRISTON

Start

Cuckmere River

P

YHA

High & Over

P

SDW

△ *Bostal Hill*

P

Bostal Bottom

Green Way

△ *Camp Hill*

△ *Norton Top*

N ←

0   ½   1   1½   2 Miles

A27

191

| Parking: | Public car park at northern end of Alfriston village (Grid ref: 521033) |
| Refreshments: | Pubs and restaurants in Alfriston. |

The Cuckmere Valley, views to the sea, the great open spaces of the South Downs, and the vast spreading acres of the Weald all help make this a truly splendid walk. Alfriston, where the walk begins is, of course, an attractive and ever-popular tourist haunt with much of interest, and you leave it by a riverside footpath which cuts behind the Clergy House, the first property bought by the National Trust. Turning away from the Cuckmere the path climbs a long grass slope to the viewpoint of High and Over from which Cuckmere Haven can be seen. There then follows a gentle airy traverse of the Downs which culminates in a lovely panorama of the Sussex Weald, before following the South Downs Way back to Alfriston.

* * *

The walk begins on the green in front of Alfriston Parish Church (1). Facing the church the thatched Clergy House (2) stands to the right. Between the two a footpath leads to the Cuckmere River where you bear right and follow the river downstream for about a mile to a

The Cuckmere River, seen from the steep climb to High and Over

footbridge that crosses to Litlington. Do not cross the river here, but continue on the right bank for another 400 yards where you cross a stile and veer right on a vague path which climbs a long grass spur to the hilltop of High and Over, seen with a white horse cut in the chalk of its east flank. As you ascend the slope be careful not to stray too far to the right where one path cuts off to the road, but keep in the pasture right to the top, gaining beautiful views over the Cuckmere's snaking course, with Cuckmere Haven (3) and the sea beyond.

Near the top of the rise cross a stile and continue up the slope between bushes and trees. The path forks. The right branch goes into a car park, but it's better to continue a little further to the summit viewpoint of High and Over (4); a glorious place with a few bench seats and an orientation table. (Grid ref: 511009)

Return from the viewpoint to the car park beside the Alfriston Road, turn right for a few paces along the road, then over a stile on the left into a sloping field. Follow the right-hand boundary (soon being joined by a bridleway emerging through a gate), and after passing through a second gate into a large open field continue ahead with a scrub slope on your right. At the end of this large field join a hedge-enclosed track which veers slightly to the right along Camp Hill, soon passing a golf course on the left. The track forks (Grid ref: 488024) with the right-hand branch offering a shorter option. Should you opt for this short-cut it forks again shortly with one route going through Greenway Bottom and rejoining the main walk just above Alfriston, the other following the track known as Green Way and coming onto the main walk again near Bostal Hill - see sketch map.

The main walk continues ahead above Blackstone Bottom, and when the hedges finish the track maintains direction over open fields with a vast panorama which includes the sea off to the left. The track then makes a gentle curve to the right above Bostal Bottom and eventually comes to the crossing route of the South Downs Way by Bopeep Bostal car park at the head of a narrow lane. Our route swings right here, but before doing so, a very short diversion is recommended. For this go ahead through a gap to enjoy a magnificent view overlooking the broad expanse of the Sussex Weald with its patchwork fields and little woodlands, and Arlington Reservoir clearly seen in the north-east, Uckfield and the blue rim of Ashdown Forest on the horizon, the rolling Downs to right and left, and Bopeep Farm just below. There are seats on the brow of the Downs to the right of the lane on which to relax and absorb the view. (Grid ref: 494051)

To resume the walk follow the trackway of the South Downs Way (5) beyond the car park and onto the crest of the Downs at Bostal Hill with expansive views once more. Over Bostal Hill the track forks with the right-hand branch being the route of the Green Way, one of the short-cut options mentioned earlier. Ignoring this continue ahead to cross another brow to gain views onto Alfriston. Sloping downhill come to a crossing track and continue ahead through bushes to join a prominent track - the route of the other short-cut alternative. Wandering down the slope you come to a residential street which leads directly to a minor crossroads by Alfriston Motors. Go ahead and shortly after come into Alfriston High Street opposite The George Inn. To return to the church bear right, for the car park go left.

Items of interest:

1: Alfriston Parish Church is dedicated to St Andrew, and dates from the 14th century. Standing on the village green, which is known as The Tye, and built in the shape of a symmetrical Greek cross, it has often been called 'The Cathedral of the Downs' on account of its imposing size.

2: The Clergy House is thought to be about the same age as the church next door. Thatched, half-timbered and set in a charming small garden, it was the first building acquired by the infant National Trust (for £10) in 1896. Seven years earlier it had so fallen into disrepair that it was due for demolition. But the then vicar, Rev. F.W. Benyon, fought hard against local apathy to stop its complete demise. He wrote: "Not a shilling has been given inside the parish to preserve the building, whilst Noah when building his ark could scarcely have been subjected to more open scorn and silent contempt for what was regarded as my hobby and my folly." Purchase by the National Trust has brought back its splendid earlier past.

3: Cuckmere Haven is the popular shingle-banked estuary of the Cuckmere River. In 1460 raiders from France sailed up the river to

Overlooking the Low Weald, from Bostal Hill

Exceat and attacked the village, which hardly exists today apart from a huddle of farm buildings and a pub. During the 18th century the Haven was a notorious landing place for smugglers when contraband goods would be brought upstream to Exceat and Alfriston. The George Inn was known then as a smuggler's haunt. In the summer of 1783, apparently, a dozen or so three-masted luggers could often be seen unloading their illicit cargoes at the same time in the Haven's shelter, and as late as 1923 smugglers were caught there with a haul of expensive brandy. Today Cuckmere Haven forms part of the Seven Sisters Country Park.

4: High and Over is one of many National Trust-owned open spaces along the South Downs. The hilltop was the site of a prehistoric burial mound in about 1000BC, while the white horse cut in the chalk just below was created in the 19th century by the farmer at nearby Frog Firle - now a youth hostel. During the war it was covered to avoid being used as a landmark by enemy bombers.

5: The South Downs Way is one of the best-loved of all long distance footpaths in Southern England, and the only National Trail that is also a bridleway. The route begins on the edge of Eastbourne and takes 102 miles to reach Winchester through some of the most spectacular lowland scenery in Britain. See *The South Downs Way & The Downs Link* by Kev Reynolds (Cicerone Press).

WALK 37
Glynde - Mount Caburn - Cliffe Hill - Glynde

Distance:	6 miles
Map:	OS Explorer 122 (17) 'South Downs Way, Steyning to Newhaven' 1:25,000
Start:	Glynde Railway Station (Grid ref: 457086)
Access:	By rail on the Lewes to Eastbourne line. By road, Glynde is located north-east of A26/A27 junction, on minor road to Ringmer.
Parking:	Public car park at entrance to Glynde Recreation Ground just north of station. (Grid ref: 457088)
Refreshments:	Pub and shop in Glynde.

A hilly circular walk which visits an Iron Age hillfort and enjoys consistently fine views throughout, whilst exploring a marooned portion of the South Downs between two spurs of the River Ouse. Glynde, where the walk begins and ends, is a small village overshadowed in repute by Glyndebourne, formerly part of the Glynde estate, but now internationally famous in the world of opera. Since refreshments are only available in Glynde itself, walkers are advised to carry a picnic lunch and something to drink. Much of the route is lacking in shelter, so on windy days make sure to have some warm clothing with you.

* * *

From the railway station cross Glynde Reach, the tidal arm of the River Ouse, and walk into the village. Just beyond the recreation ground turn left into Ranscombe Lane, and a few paces after passing Glynde Stores, cross a stile on the right and follow a footpath rising gently through three interlinking fields. The upper field is a tremendous wild flower meadow in spring and early summer. On reaching the crown of the hill turn left immediately in front of a stile in order to visit Mount Caburn, but note that you'll return to this stile later to continue the walk. (Grid ref: 445093)

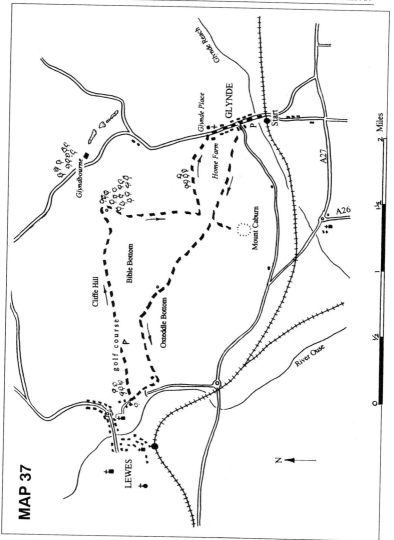

The path leads directly onto the brow of Mount Caburn (1), which has a bench seat on the southern side from which to enjoy a lovely view over the River Ouse (2). Return to the path junction at the stile, bear left to cross it and wander downhill through a large open field to a narrow cleave, or valley. In the bed of this, steep slopes fold one against another. On coming to a concrete dew pond (3) in Oxteddle Bottom, go a few paces beyond and then veer left. Marker posts then direct the route up the opposite slope to another stile. Over this turn sharp left. In a few paces the way forks. The left-hand option goes to Southerham Farm, while ours gently ascends the slope ahead above another coombe and, rising along the flank of the Downs, crosses more stiles. After negotiating a stile in the right-hand corner of a field near the clubhouse of Lewes Golf Club, the way veers right into a small car park. (Grid ref: 426099)

Walk down the drive, from which you have views onto Lewes (4), with the golf course stretching to the right. Before long the gradient steepens and, immediately before coming to the first house, turn right onto a track, and a few paces later break off on a footpath, also on the right, to ascend a flight of steps among trees. All the height that was lost on the descent from the clubhouse has to be regained. Come onto the golf course to the right of an obelisk. Waymark posts clearly show the way across the golf course, informing you too of the direction from which golfers will be driving. Beware flying golf balls. Eventually come to a stile leading off the golf course below the unseen summit of Cliffe Hill. (Grid ref: 435105)

Walk directly ahead across the southern flank of Cliffe Hill, passing through two adjoining fields from which you can see the dew pond below in Oxteddle Bottom. Whilst crossing the second field you pass above earthworks of Bible Bottom, so-named because they have the vague appearance of an open book. At the end of the second field cross another stile where a low marker stone is known as Saxon Cross. Views from this downland crest are to the north, with Ringmer lying in the flat bed of the Low Weald. Maintain direction along a grass trail which passes to the right of a woodland. Beyond this the way slopes downhill to a second concrete dew pond on the edge of another wood. (Grid ref: 446106)

Just past the dew pond there's a crossing track. (A gate on the left takes this track down to the road linking Glynde with Ringmer.) Turn sharp right on the track, a licensed footpath, which cuts along the east slope of Saxon Down and passes what appears to be a small chalk quarry. A few paces beyond this the track forks. Take the left branch and soon come to a stile beside a field gate. Over this wander ahead on a grass path along the crest of the Downs, with Mount Caburn coming into view straight ahead. On reaching a track breaking off to the left, leave the Caburn route and follow this as it eases downhill, with lovely views for much of the way, until coming to the road by Home Farm at the northern end of Glynde (5). (Grid ref: 455094) Turn right and wander down into the village, passing Glynde Place (6) and the parish church as you do.

Items of interest:

1: Mount Caburn, or The Caburn, as the Ordnance Survey has it, clearly shows two defensive dikes and the earthen ramparts of a one-time hillfort built in the third century BC by one of the Celtic tribes that occupied this part of the Downs. It is thought that about seventy families lived on this elevated site, which stands some 492 feet above sea level, and a number of archaeological discoveries made at the site may now be studied in Lewes Museum. Needless to say, there's a splendid panoramic view overlooking the final writhings of the River Ouse in one direction, and the vast levels of the Low Weald in the other. Mount Caburn is a protected nature reserve.

2: The River Ouse used to spill into the English Channel at Seaford. In those days Seaford was the port for Lewes, but a great storm in 1579 changed the course of the river and it found a 'new haven' a little to the west - the Newhaven of today.

3: Dew ponds are found throughout the South Downs. Conscious of the permeable nature of chalk, farmers originally dug out saucer-shaped scoops which were then given a clay base to trap and retain rain water for their livestock. Most dew ponds seen today are lined with concrete.

4: Lewes commands the Ouse valley, and had one of the earliest Norman castles, built by William de Warenne, who was given the Rape of Lewes by William the Conqueror. Although the stronghold was built to protect the town against invaders sailing up the Ouse estuary, the castle was never really put to the test. In May 1264 the Battle of Lewes, between Henry III's men and those of Simon de Montfort, took place on the South Downs west of the town. Such was the carnage, that when navvies were digging the railway in 1846, they came upon a mass grave of those who were slaughtered nearly 600 years before, the bones of whom filled thirteen waggons. Lewes is basically medieval in layout, but it was heavily altered in Georgian times. Daniel Defoe described it as "a fine pleasant town, well built, agreeably situated in the middle of an open champaign country." He also praised its situation, which he thought "the most romantic I ever saw". A century later, in 1822, William Cobbet found the town to be "a model of solidity and neatness … the people well-dressed; and, though last not least, the girls remarkably pretty." It is, of course, the county town of East Sussex.

5: Glynde Its name comes from *gline*, which means 'a fenced enclosure' - presumably a reference to the fortified site of Mount Caburn. As far as architecture is concerned, the village would pass without remark were it not for the Palladian style of the parish church. Standing next to Glynde Place (see below) the church of St Mary the Virgin was built on the site of an earlier medieval place of worship in 1763-65 by Bishop Richard Trevor who lived next door. The architect, Sir Thomas Robinson, had recently returned from Italy enthusiastic for the Renaissance buildings he'd seen there, hence the style which is quite out of keeping with its downland setting. Inside the building a series of fine stained glass windows have been erected as memorials to the first Viscount Hampden and his family, while the walls are hung with arabesque-styled hessian. As for Glyndebourne, up the road a short distance, it was opened as an opera house in 1934 by John and Audrey Christie, and has now gained an international reputation, as much for its setting as for the quality of the performances.

6: Glynde Place, which is open to the public on summer weekends, stands back from the road and is approached through the stables. The house itself is a noted Elizabethan building of flint construction, originally with the entrance to the west to face the road, but turned back-to-front in the 18th century in order to face across a parkland to the east.

WALK 38
Ditchling - Lower Standean - Ditchling

Distance:	8 miles
Map:	OS Explorer 122 (17) 'South Downs Way, Steyning to Newhaven' 1:25,000
Start:	Ditchling crossroads (Grid ref: 326153)
Access:	Nearest railway station at Hassocks, 1½ miles west. Ditchling is at the junction of B2116 and B2112, south-east of Burgess Hill.
Parking:	Free public car park at rear of Ditchling Village Hall 100 yards east of crossroads.
Refreshments:	Pubs and shops in Ditchling.

From the attractive village of Ditchling the South Downs can be seen as a steep wall rising abruptly from low-lying meadows grazed by horses. Climbing the north flank of the Downs, the walk tackles the slope of Burnhouse Bostall to gain a tremendous panorama that includes the patchwork patterns of the Weald, the blue hint of distant Ashdown Forest and, to south, east and west, the Downs themselves. Following the route of the South Downs Way westward, we visit the Clayton Windmills (Jack and Jill), before heading south away from the scarp edge into the folding heartland of the Downs, then curving east above the farm buildings of Lower Standean. The circuit is maintained through the wooded grove of North Bottom, rises along the edge of Heathy Brow to the high point of Ditchling Beacon, before plunging downhill back to Ditchling once more. This is a rewarding but energetic circuit with plenty of ups and downs to contend with.

*   *   *

From the crossroads in Ditchling (1) near the church, walk along South Street (the B2112), in the direction of Brighton, and when the road forks after about 150 yards go directly ahead on a fence-enclosed footpath which leads to a small residential estate. The continuing footpath breaks off to the right by the side of Neville Flats and enters a field. Bear left and soon pass between hedgerows heavy with dog roses in early summer. The path is clearly signed, and after edging one or two fields, comes to the buildings of Park Barn Farm and goes between barns to the farm drive opposite a row

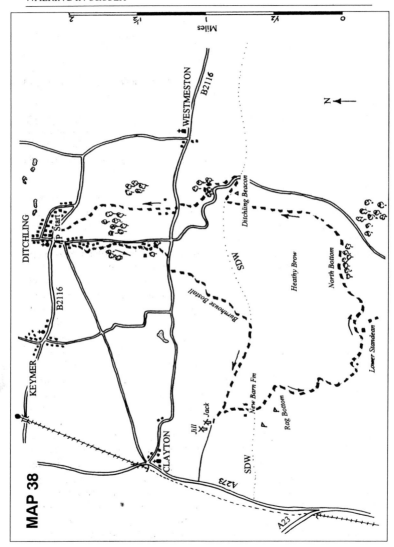

MAP 38

of stables. At the left-hand end of these the way enters woodland. Through this cross a meadow to the far corner where you come onto the aptly-named Underhill Lane. (Grid ref: 324138)

Turn right for about 200 yards, as far as a trackway cutting left and signposted to Patcham. The way soon narrows to footpath dimensions and begins to ascend the downland slope among trees, then out to the open grassland of Burnhouse Bostall with its view into the narrow groove of Coombe Bottom. On gaining the crest of the Downs come to a fence and a gate, on the other side of which a crossing track is part of the South Downs Way. (2) Bear right to reach Keymer Post, a tall oak signpost which marks the boundaries of West and East Sussex. (Grid ref: 315129) Brighton can be seen sprawling in the distance to the left.

Remain on the South Downs Way heading north-west with the Downs stretching far ahead as an extended buttress to the Weald's low acres. At a gate where the way forks, continue directly ahead, and about 100 yards before reaching the Clayton Windmills (3), the South Downs Way breaks away left at a junction of tracks. Alhough they're slightly off our route it is worth taking the right-hand option as far as the windmills. (Grid ref: 303134) The first, known as Jack, is privately owned, but 'Jill' is often open to the public on summer weekends. Given clear visibility, the slope just below 'Jill' makes a fine viewpoint.

From the windmills return to the South Downs Way track junction and veer right (south) wandering towards New Barn Farm. Just beyond the farm come to crosstracks where the South Downs Way goes off to the right. Here we leave this long distance path and continue directly ahead with a golf course on the right. The track slopes down to Rag Bottom (masses of poppies line the way in summer) and rises again on the far side. Over the brow of the hill the track forks. Bear left between large open fields, and on coming to a line of trees go through a gate on the right and wander alongside the trees. The path soon swings left on the edge of another field. On the far side of this curve left to a gateway down the slope, then go through to a track which passes to the left of a brick barn. Immediately before reaching the farm buildings of Lower Standean turn left on another, more narrow, track heading for Heathy Brow. Passing through a couple of gates, the way swings round the downland slope and descends to another, more obvious, track. (Grid ref: 318116)

A short distance along this go through a gate into the right-hand field, then bear left through the middle of the field, curving into North Bottom with a woodland above to the right. The faint grass path leads through a second field, and at its upper left-hand corner, passes through a gateway and continues uphill on a track, ignoring other paths breaking from it. As you progress, so the panorama increases, displaying a vast rolling countryside of great charm, serenaded by countless skylarks. Eventually gain the crossing path of the South Downs Way again, with Ditchling seen ahead far below. Bear right, pass just below the trig point which marks Ditchling Beacon (4) and come to a car park beside the Ditchling Road. (Grid ref: 333131) (There's often an ice cream van parked here - a treat to those of us who are ice creamaholics!)

Cross the road (note the dew pond ahead) and walk down it for about 50 yards to find a path which soon plunges down the slope among trees. At the foot of the slope continue ahead to a crossing lane (Underhill Lane once more) where you turn left, and about 100 yards later bear right into Nye Lane. This becomes a track and forks. Take the left-hand option, sloping downhill slightly among trees. On coming to double gates go through these and continue ahead to a concrete drive. When this cuts sharply left continue ahead, now on a footpath alongside Jointer Copse, and when the path forks by a small pond, veer left. Forty yards on it forks again. This time take the right-hand option. When it forks yet again, cross a stile on the left into a meadow, while the main path continues directly ahead to Ditchling. For a short distance the two paths run parallel, but having crossed a second stile, we now aim towards Ditchling church, whose spire can be clearly seen. The way crosses through three fields, then between hedges on a grass path, to a driveway which leads directly to the B2116. Bear left and you'll soon be at the crossroads in the heart of Ditchling where the walk began.

Items of interest:

1: Ditchling has many attractive and interesting buildings, a number of which are walled with flint. The church dates from the 13th century and stands above West Street. From 1541 until her death in

1557, the patron was Anne of Cleves, who lived in what is now Wings Place opposite the church gate. Formerly known as Anne of Cleves House, Wings Place is a romantic Tudor timber and brick manor house. There's a small museum to the west of the church.

2: The South Downs Way links Eastbourne and Winchester by 102 miles of footpath and trackway, and is one of the finest long distance walking routes in southern England. Initially opened in 1972 when the route finished in Buriton on the Hampshire border (it was extended to Winchester in 1987), it's the only National Trail that is also a bridleway throughout its length. See *The South Downs Way & The Downs Link* by Kev Reynolds (Cicerone Press).

3: The Clayton Windmills are a well-known feature of the South Downs. Black-painted 'Jack' is a smock mill built in 1866, but it has since been converted to a private residence and was once the home of golfer, Henry Longhurst, while 'Jill' - the lower, wooden post mill - is in the care of a preservation society (The Jack and Jill Windmills Society) and is open to the public most weekends between May and September. Originally built in 1821, 'Jill' formerly stood in Patcham, Brighton, but was towed to her present position by teams of oxen, where she worked until 1909. From the car park on the western side of 'Jill' a footpath descends the slope to the hamlet of Clayton on the A273.

4: Ditchling Beacon at 813 feet is the highest point of this section of the South Downs, and was once described by Richard Jeffries (in *Nature Near London*) as "the nearest and the most accessible of the southern Alps from London". A beacon used to stand here as one of a series that would be lit to warn of invasion. It is said that the light of a beacon burning here could be seen from Seaford to the east, and also from the North Downs. The site was adopted for a hillfort during the Iron Age, and the rectangular grassy ramparts of that defence can still be made out.

WALK 39
Washington - Chanctonbury Ring - Washington

Distance:	4³/₄ miles
Map:	OS Explorer 121 'Arundel & Pulborough' 1:25,000
Start:	Washington Car Park (Grid ref: 120120)
Access:	By bus from Worthing. Washington lies just off A24/A283 junction.
Parking:	Public car park at foot of Downs, south of village.
Refreshments:	Pub in Washington.

Chanctonbury Ring is one of the best-known features of the South Downs, a prominent clump of beech and sycamore trees planted on the four-acre site of an Iron Age hillfort, that is seen from many distant parts of Sussex. Sadly, the Great Storm of October 1987 decimated the Ring, but it still remains a proud symbol of the Downs and an obvious destination for a walk. On this circuit we start and finish by the attractive, typically downland village of Washington, wander along the base of the Downs, then climb through woodland to the open crest south-east of Chanctonbury Ring and follow the route of the South Downs Way to, and beyond, the Ring, before descending back to Washington. As with all our South Downs walks, huge views make this another memorable outing.

*   *   *

From the entrance to Washington Car Park walk along a track (footpath sign) heading north. When it curves right continue ahead on a more narrow track/drive which serves a few houses. At a multi-junction of tracks cut left to descend round a bend among trees, and wander on to the former main road. Pass The Street on your left (to visit Washington Church (1) divert along this for a short distance) and about 50 yards later, cross a stile on the right to a footpath which shortly climbs a series of steps. Veering right into a field wander along the left-hand edge parallel with the wooded slopes of the Downs. About 100 yards from the end of the field an oak post directs the path half-right across the corner, through a gap in a dividing hedge into the next field, where you maintain direction towards the far corner. Big views stretch north across the Weald, while the windmill standing on Rock Common outside Washington

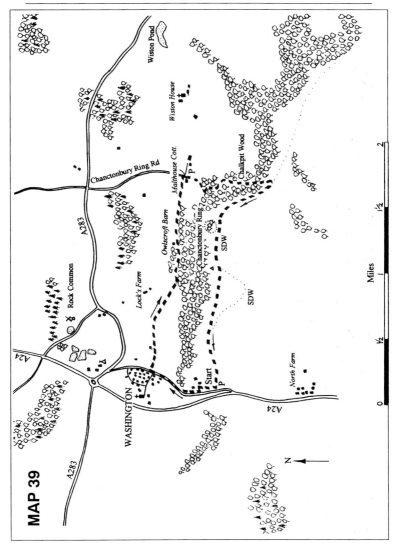

MAP 39

Wiston Pond

Wiston House

Chanctonbury Ring Rd

Malthouse Cott.

Chalkpit Wood

A283

Owlscroft Barn

Rock Common

Lock's Farm

Chanctonbury Ring

SDW

SDW

A24

Start

P

North Farm

WASHINGTON

A283

A24

N

0   ½   1   ½   2

Miles

makes a prominent focus. At the foot of the woodland slope there's a junction of paths. (Grid ref: 133125)

That which cuts back to the right offers a short but steep route to Chanctonbury Ring, but we go ahead on a bridleway which at first edges the woods, then rises pleasantly among trees before sloping down again to pass alongside Owlscroft Barn, an old corrugated building with a rust-red roof. A broad, heavily rutted track takes the route forward, and I should imagine this could be pretty muddy at times. On emerging from the woods the continuing Downs can be seen far ahead beyond the Adur's breach at Steyning. Eventually come to Malthouse Cottage and a narrow crossing lane -Chanctonbury Ring Road. Turn right and walk towards the South Downs and a small car parking area. (Grid ref: 145124)

A track leads on, winding through the woods, steadily climbing the steep north flank. This route is shown on the OS map as Wiston Bostal. Near the head of the slope the track is little more than a pair of parallel footpaths, and on emerging from the woods you come to the major crossing track of the South Downs Way. Turn right and, rising gently, Chanctonbury Ring soon comes into view ahead. (2) (Grid ref: 139120) A superb panorama rewards the approach - the coast is clearly seen in one direction, the extensive Weald in the other.

Pass along the left-hand side of the Ring. Immediately beyond it a path on the right is the short-cut option met at the foot of the slope. Continue along the South Downs Way which soon veers leftwards below the trig point marking the summit of Chanctonbury Hill (781ft). Go through a gateway, then leave the main track and veer right through a gate onto a broad fenced meadow. Cross this heading west along the crest of the Downs, then slope down to another gate in the lower fence with Washington seen in the valley below. Through this the trail weaves among humps and pits before rejoining the South Downs Way which has made a curious dog-leg since we left it. Ignoring alternative path options remain on the SDW which leads to Washington Car Park.

Items of interest:

1: Washington Church stands at the end of The Street beyond a row of attractive flint and brick-built cottages. Dedicated to St Mary the building, with the exception of the solid-looking tower and the 13th century columns and arches of the north arcade, was pulled down in 1866 and rebuilt from the foundations. The first parish church is thought to have been built in the 12th century, but this was replaced by another by the Knights Templar, to which the present tower was added in the reign of Henry VII.

2: Chanctonbury Ring historically refers to the Iron Age hillfort site which contains a Romano-Celtic temple of the 3rd or 4th centuries. It is assumed that there were links with nearby Cissbury Ring, another fort of the same period across the Downs to the south. The clump of beech and sycamores that adorns the site was planted in 1760 by Charles Goring of Wiston House, seen below to the north-east. Those trees that were uprooted by the 1987 storm have been cleared away and replacements planted. The Ring is now fenced to protect the young trees. Views from Chanctonbury are far-reaching and justifiably well-known.

WALK 40
Findon - Cissbury Ring - Findon

Distance:	7¼ miles
Map:	OS Explorer 121 'Arundel & Pulborough' 1:25,000
Start:	The Square, Findon (Grid ref: 122088)
Access:	By bus from Worthing, Horsham and Midhurst. Findon is located about 4 miles north of Worthing, off A24.
Parking:	No day-long public parking in Findon, but small car park below Cissbury Ring (Grid ref: 139085) - in which case begin walk there.
Refreshments:	Pubs, cafés and shop in Findon. None on the walk.

South of Chanctonbury Ring the Downs are used by farmers as a mixture of arable and grazing; it's a vast open landscape of almost treeless hills folding one after another, with waterless valleys between them, the only shade on hot summer days thrown at best by low-growing scrub. Footpaths, bridleways and ancient trackways strike across the land. They follow ridgetops and sneak along the bed of tight little valleys - enough trails to allow a variety of circuits to be made. Racehorses are put through their paces on chalk tracks and downland acres, and the gleam of the sea sparkles in southward views. It is an ancient land, of that there is no doubt, and both the huge Iron Age hillfort of Cissbury Ring (one of the largest in the country), and the nearby flint mines, testify to its occupation by man for more than 2000 years - although today any habitation away from its fringe is sparse indeed.

*   *   *

From the crossroads in the heart of Findon by The Gunn Inn walk down The Square and bear left into Stable Lane (signpost to Chanctonbury). The lane rises gently between houses and brings

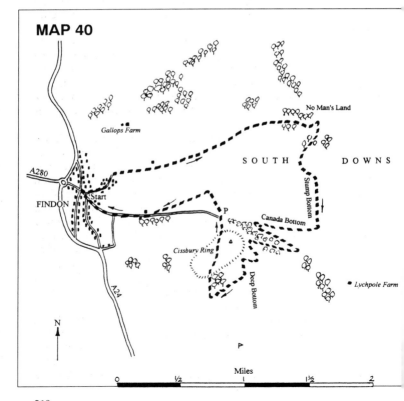

MAP 40

you to the upper edge of the village where it ends. Directly ahead a drive goes to Gallops Farm, while a track cuts away to the right, leading onto the crest of the Downs. This is the route to take.

Wandering up the slope the trees marking Chanctonbury Ring can be seen away to the left, while the English Channel glimmers beyond the urban cluster of Worthing to the right. About a third of a mile from Stable Lane you pass a lone white house standing back on the left. This is the last habitation on the walk until you return to Findon. Half a mile beyond this come to four-way crosstracks. (Grid ref: 139094) The left-hand route leads to Chanctonbury Ring and the South Downs Way, the right-hand option is a direct way to Cissbury Ring, while we continue ahead on a slightly more narrow track than that which has brought us this far.

An immense downland panorama unfolds as you wander. In summer larks rise to minute specks in the sky, their trilling song giving voice to the landscape. But in winter the land is stark and grey, and arctic winds cut across the hills without check. Imagine how this must have seemed to our Iron Age ancestors who bore those winters in rough shelters with neither central heating nor double-glazed protection!

As the track slopes downhill towards No Man's Land it forks. Veer right and continue through scrub to the foot of the slope where a bridleway cuts sharply back to the right. Keep ahead on what is part of the Monarch's Way (1) for a few paces, then turn right when the track forks. The way soon goes between two lines of scrub-like trees, then edges along the foot of a large sloping field through what is known as Stump Bottom. At the far end of the field come to a crossing track and bear right. (Grid ref: 151083) Fences lead the way between fields through Canada Bottom, and about 40 yards after passing a barn, go through a gate on the left and walk along the bottom edge of National Trust land. On coming to a second gate, do not pass through it, but instead cut sharply back to the right on a path which angles up the slope among scrub.

Almost at the head of the slope come to a crossing path/track and go through a gate on the left (the third such gate up this slope). The outer earthen ramparts of Cissbury Ring (2) rise nearby, and although our route ignores the site at this point (but will pass right through later), you may prefer to explore the Ring before continuing with the walk.

After passing through the gate walk ahead on a track with the ramparts to your right. The track becomes more profound as it approaches a field gate, but swings to the right without going through. Remain on the chalk track as it slopes downhill below and to the south of Cissbury Ring. Passing round the head of Deep Bottom the track rises again to another gate. Through this there's a fine oak finger post offering directions to Findon ($^1/_2$ mile), Findon Valley ($^1/_2$ mile), Worthing (1 mile) and, the way we've just come, Steyning Bowl (2 miles). Ignoring all these directions bear hard right and walk up a gentle slope alongside a fence and after going through yet another gate, enter Cissbury Ring. (Grid ref: 138077)

Cross through the Ring on a grass path. When it forks take the left-hand option (the right path leads to a trig point). The way leads to the northern ramparts (giving glorious views), then descends steps, crosses a track or two and comes to a small parking area at the head of a narrow lane. (Grid ref: 139085) **Note: If you arrived by car, this is where the walk should begin.**

Cross through the car park and continue ahead on a track between large fields. At the end of the first field section, you will find a narrow crossing bridleway. This is also part of the Monarch's Way briefly visited earlier. Turn left and follow this down a slope to a lane where you bear right. When you come to a crossing lane continue ahead along Nepcote Lane. This leads directly to The Square in Findon (3) and the end of the walk.

Items of interest:

1: The Monarch's Way is a 609-mile long distance walk based on the route taken in 1651 by Charles II following the Battle of Worcester. Starting in Worcester it visits Stratford-upon-Avon, the Cotswolds, Mendips and along the south coast from Dorset to Sussex, where it ends at Shoreham. (See *The Monarch's Way* by Trevor Anthill published in three paperbacks by Meridian Books.)

2: Cissbury Ring is the largest and most impressive of all the earthworks on the South Downs, covering no less than 65 acres. There are two clearly defined ramparts of this Iron Age hillfort, dating from about 300 to 59 BC, and it has been estimated that about 60,000 tons of chalk had to be dug from the ditch in order to build them. Flint mining was carried out in the New Stone Age (4300-3500 BC) long before the hillfort was built, and shafts up to 40ft deep, leading to galleries, have been discovered here. Even a quick examination of the site shows a whole series of mounds and depressions which tell of this mining activity, which would suggest that Cissbury was one of southern England's major flint mining sites. Before the Roman occupation (AD43) it appears to have been abandoned as a fortification, but it was reoccupied towards the end of the Roman period, presumably against attack from the Saxons. Views from the outer ramparts are magnificent, and include Selsey Bill and the Isle of Wight, and the spire of Chichester Cathedral.

3: Findon has an annual sheep fair which first took place in the 13th century, and is now held on the second Saturday of September. It's a pleasant village with a number of flint houses and walls typical of the Downs, and with the Downs crowding on both sides of its valley. Cut off from the village by the busy A24, the flint-built parish church of St John the Baptist stands 1/2 mile to the west, near the 18th century Findon Place.

*   *   *

LONG DISTANCE PATHS

A number of long distance walking routes pass through Sussex which may appeal to users of this guide. Most of these have been developed or promoted by bodies like the Countryside Commission, the Ramblers' Association, County or District Councils. All lead through charming country and are worth considering, should you be interested in the idea of walking day after day.

The majority of these routes have been created by linking existing rights of way wherever possible. Most will have no individual form of waymarking, and it will be necessary to study the recommended guidebook to follow the route throughout. But some do have their own identifying symbol which appears on finger posts, stiles and gates; for example the acorn sign of a National Trail which indicates the route of the South Downs Way, and the WW letters of the Wealdway.

Tackling a multi-day route can be a very rewarding experience, and there can be few finer ways of getting to the very heart of the countryside. Day after day the journey leads through an ever-changing landscape, giving an insight to the rich diversity that is rural Sussex. Some routes follow a specific topographical feature, such as the South Downs, while others cross a whole series of hills against the grain of the land, with all the changes of vegetation that this entails.

The following list of LDPs in Sussex gives only the briefest of details, but anyone wishing to find out more about a particular route, will find mention of the guidebook or route leaflets available.

1: THE SOUTH DOWNS WAY

Distance:	102 miles
Start:	Eastbourne *Finish:* Winchester, Hampshire
Guidebooks:	*The South Downs Way & The Downs Link* by Kev Reynolds (Cicerone Press) *South Downs Way* by Paul Millmore (Aurum Press)
	A Guide to the South Downs Way by Miles Jebb (Constable)

A very popular National Trail that is also a bridleway. From

Eastbourne there's a choice of routes as far as Alfriston; one climbs to Beachy Head and crosses the Seven Sisters to Cuckmere Haven, the inland option visits Jevington. Thereafter the SDW traces the northern escarpment of the Downs with splendid views across the Weald. When the South Downs Way first opened, it went only as far as Buriton on the Hampshire border, but has since been extended as far as Winchester.

2: THE WEALDWAY

Distance: 82 miles
Start: Gravesend (Kent)   *Finish:* Beachy Head
Guidebooks: *The Wealdway & The Vanguard Way* by Kev Reynolds (Cicerone Press) *Along & Around The Wealdway* by Helen Livingston (KCC & ESCC)

From the River Thames to the English Channel the Wealdway cuts through the back-country of the North Downs, then descends the scarp slope to join the River Medway which it follows into Tonbridge. From there the WW crosses a series of High Weald ridges, then enters East Sussex to climb over Ashdown Forest. South of the Forest the way continues through farmland before crossing the Low Weald and, finally, onto the South Downs to Beachy Head. A very fine walk which makes an exploration of the Weald of Kent and Sussex.

3: THE VANGUARD WAY

Distance: 66 miles
Start: East Croydon (Greater London)   *Finish:* Newhaven
Guidebooks: *The Vanguard Way* (Vanguards Rambling Club, c/o 109 Selsdon Park Road, South Croydon CR2 8JJ) *The Wealdway & The Vanguard Way* by Kev Reynolds (Cicerone Press)

Similar in concept to the Wealdway, the Vanguard Way links the London suburbs with the English Channel. Devised by members of the Croydon-based Vanguards Rambling Club in 1980, the VW soon escapes suburbia and descends the North Downs escarpment, crosses the Greensand Ridge on the Kent-Surrey border, then strikes south through the Weald to Forest Row and Ashdown Forest. Across the Forest heathland to Blackboys Youth Hostel, then through the Low Weald to the Cuckmere Valley at Alfriston. The final stage follows the Cuckmere to Seaford Head, then along the coast to Newhaven Harbour.

4: HIGH WEALD WALK

Distance:	28 miles
Start/Finish:	Southborough Common (Kent)
Guidebook:	*Along & Around The High Weald Walk* by Bea Cowan (KCC)

This circular walk makes a ring through the countryside surrounding Tunbridge Wells, passing through a corner of East Sussex as it does. Much of the way is in the High Weald Area of Outstanding Natural Beauty, with its rich variety of scenery.

5: HIGH WEALD LANDSCAPE TRAIL

Distance:	90 miles
Start:	Horsham *Finish:* Rye
Guide:	*High Weald Landscape Trail - (KCC)*

Launched in July 1999, the High Weald Landscape Trail makes a meandering route across the Sussex Weald from west to east. The western section of about 35 miles between Horsham and East Grinstead was waymarked first. Leading through some very fine scenery it links with five recommended circular walks.

6: THE SUSSEX BORDER PATH

Distance:	150 miles
Start:	Emsworth (Hants) *Finish:* Rye
Guidebook:	*Sussex Border Path* by Ben Perkins & Aeneas Mackintosh (Dr Ben Perkins, 11 Old London Road, Brighton BN1 8XR)

Wherever possible this long route traces footpaths along the county boundaries, but it also strays into Hampshire, Kent and Surrey. The mid-Sussex link of 38 miles cuts away from the main Border Path at East Grinstead and heads south more or less following the administrative border between East and West Sussex. Several walks included in the present volume touch upon paths adopted by the SBP.

7: THE DOWNS LINK

Distance:	37 miles
Start:	St Martha's Hill (Surrey) *Finish:* Shoreham-by-Sea
Guidebook: .	*The South Downs Way & The Downs Link* by Kev Reynolds (Cicerone Press)

Ideal for a weekend's walk, as its name suggests the Downs Link journeys between the North Downs Way and the South Downs Way, for the most part along the trackbed of two abandoned railways. The sandy crown of St Martha's Hill overlooks a lovely wooded landscape, and the initial stretch of the walk winds through woodland before joining the former Horsham and Guildford line near Cranleigh. The southern part of the walk follows the old Itchingfield Junction to Shoreham line through Partridge Green and Bramber.

8: THE WEY-SOUTH PATH

Distance:	36 miles
Start:	Guildford (Surrey) *Finish:* Amberley
Guide:	*The Wey-South Path* (leaflet from W&A Enterprises Ltd., 24 Griffiths Avenue, Lancing, West Sussex BN15 0HW)

Following the towpath of the Godalming Navigation from Guildford, the River Wey leads to the Wey & Arun Junction Canal. It is not possible to keep to the old towpath throughout, but paths, roads and a disused railway enable the walk to link with the River Arun beside which it continues to Amberley. (See The Arun Way below)

9: THE ARUN WAY

Distance:	22 miles
Start:	Littlehampton *Finish:* Pulborough
Guidebook:	*Along the Arun* by John Adamson (Alexius Press, 114 Sandhurst Road, Kingsbury, London NW9 9LN)

As its title suggests, this route wanders through the picturesque Lower Arun Valley and links with the Wey-South Path at Amberley.

10: THE LIPCHIS WAY

Distance:	26 miles
Start:	Liphook (Hants)
Finish:	Chichester
Guide:	*The Lipchis Way* (leaflet from Liphook Ramblers, c/o 21 Chestnut Close, Liphook, Hants GU30 7JA)

This route, which was opened in 1985, takes in the western Weald with its heathland, woods and farmland, then crosses the South Downs on the final leg to Chichester.

11: 1066 COUNTRY WALK

Distance:	31 miles
Start:	Rye
Finish:	Alfriston
Guide:	*1066 Country Walk* (leaflet from Rother District Council, Town Hall, Bexhill on Sea TN39 3JX)

Linking sites of historical interest, the walk inevitably goes through Battle on its route west to Alfriston. There are connections with the Saxon Shore Way and South Downs Way, and a link route to Hastings.

*   *   *

APPENDIX A
Useful Addresses

1: East Sussex County Council
Rights of Way & Countryside
Management
Transport & Environment
Department
Sackville House
LEWES BN7 1UE

2: West Sussex County Council
County Planning Department
Tower Street
CHICHESTER PO19 1RL

3: Sussex Downs Conservation
Board
Chanctonbury House
Church Street
STORRINGTON RH20 4LT

4: Countryside Agency
South East Regional Office
71 Kingsway
LONDON C2B 6ST

5: The National Trust
(Kent & East Sussex Regional
Office)
Scotney Castle
LAMBERHURST Kent

6: The Ramblers' Association
1-5 Wandsworth Road
LONDON SW8 2LJ

7: English Heritage
23 Saville Row
LONDON W1X 1AB

8: South-East England Tourist
Board
1 Warwick Park
TUNBRIDGE WELLS
Kent TN2 5TA

9: Southern England Tourist Board
40 Chamberlayne Road
EASTLEIGH
Hants SO5 5JH

10: Society of Sussex Downsmen
93 Church Road
HOVE
BN3 2BA

11: High Weald Unit
Corner Farm
Hastings Road
FLIMWELL
East Sussex TN5 7PR

Tourist Information Centres

1: 61 High Street
ARUNDEL
W. Sussex BN18 9AJ
(01903 882268)

2: Belmont Street
BOGNOR REGIS
W. Sussex PO21 1BJ
(01243 823140)

3: 10 Bartholomew Square
BRIGHTON
E. Sussex BN1 1JS
(01273 292599)

4: 29A South Street
CHICHESTER
W. Sussex PO19 1AH
(01243 775888)

5: Cornfield Road
EASTBOURNE
E. Sussex BN21 4LQ
(01323 411400)

6: Little Chef Complex
FONTWELL
Arundel
W. Sussex BN18 0SD
(01243 543269)

7: The Library
Western Road
HAILSHAM
E. Sussex BN27 3DN
(01323 844426)

8: King Alfred Leisure Centre
Church Road
HOVE
E. Sussex BN3 3BQ
(01273 292589)

9: 187 High Street
LEWES
E. Sussex BN7 2DE
(01273 483448)

10: Windmill Complex
Seafront
The Green
LITTLEHAMPTON
W. Sussex BN17 5EP
(01903 713480)

11: Pevensey Castle
PEVENSEY
E. Sussex BN24 5LE
(01323 761444)

12: 25 Clinton Place
SEAFORD
E. Sussex BN25 1NP
(01323 897426)

13: Town Hall
Chapel Road
WORTHING
W. Sussex BN11 1HL
(01903 210022)

APPENDIX B

Recommended Further Reading

	Illustrated Guide to Britain (AA/Drive Publications, 1974)
Arscott, David	*Sussex: The County in Colour* (The Dovecote Press, 1995)
Belloc, Hilaire	*The Four Men* (London, 1912)
	The County of Sussex (London, 1936)
Christian, Garth	*Ashdown Forest* (Society of the Friends of Ashdown Forest, 1967)
Cobbett, William	*Rural Rides* (London, 1830)
Godfrey, John	*Sussex, the New Shell Guides* (Michael Joseph, 1990)
Hudson, W.H.	*Nature in Downland* (London, 1900)
Jefferies, Richard	*Nature Near London* (London, 1893/John Clare Books, 1980)
	The Open Air (London, 1885)
Kaye-Smith, S.	*Weald of Kent & Sussex* (Robert Hale, 1953)
Mason, Oliver	*South-East England* (Bartholomew, 1979)
Nairn, I. & Pevsner, N.	*The Buildings of England: Sussex* (Penguin Books, 1965)
Reynolds, Kev	*Classic Walks in Southern England* (Oxford Illustrated Press, 1990)
Sankey, John	*Nature Guide to South-East England* (Usborne, 1981)
Seward, Desmond	*Sussex* (Pimlico/Random House, 1995)
Spence, Keith	*The Companion Guide to Kent & Sussex* (Collins, 1973)

CICERONE GUIDES to Walking and Cycling in Southern England

SOUTH & SOUTH WEST Long Distance Trails

THE KENNET & AVON WALK *Ray Quinlan* 90 miles along riverside and canal, from Westminster to Avonmouth, full of history, wildlife, delectable villages and pubs. *ISBN 1 85284 090 0 200pp*

THE SOUTHERN COAST-TO-COAST WALK *Ray Quinlan* The equivalent of the popular northern walk. 283 miles from Weston-super-Mare to Dover. *ISBN 1 85284 117 6 200pp*

SOUTH WEST WAY - A Walker's Guide to the Coast Path *Martin Collins*
Vol.1 Minehead to Penzance *ISBN 1 85284 025 0   184pp   PVC cover*
Vol.2 Penzance to Poole *Martin Collins   ISBN 1 85284 026 9   198pp   PVC cover*
Two volumes which cover the spectacular coastal path around Britain's south-west peninsula. Profusely illustrated. Full of practical detail.

THE THAMES PATH *Leigh Hatts* Described from the Thames Barrier to the source, the most rewarding way of doing the walk. *ISBN 1 85284 270 9 184pp*

THE TWO MOORS WAY *James Roberts* 100 miles crossing Dartmoor, the delightful villages of central Devon and Exmoor to the rugged coast at Lynmouth. *ISBN 1 85284 159 1 100pp*

THE WEALDWAY & THE VANGUARD WAY *Kev Reynolds* Two long distance walks in Kent, from the outskirts of London to the coast. *ISBN 0 902363 85 9 160pp*

SOUTHERN & SOUTH EAST ENGLAND

CANAL WALKS Vol 3 South *Dennis Needham ISBN 1 85284 227 X 176pp*

CHANNEL ISLAND WALKS *Paddy Dillon* 47 one day walks on this wonderful holiday isle, with easy bus and boat services. *ISBN 1 85284 288 1*

WALKING IN THE CHILTERNS *Duncan Unsworth*
35 short circular walks in this area of woods and little valleys with cosy pubs and old churches. *ISBN 1 85284 127 3 184pp*

A WALKER'S GUIDE TO THE ISLE OF WIGHT *Martin Collins & Norman Birch* The best walks on this sunshine island, including short circuits and longer trails. *ISBN 1 85284 221 0 216 pp*

WALKING IN KENT Vol I *Kev Reynolds ISBN 1 85284 192 3 200pp*

WALKING IN KENT Vol II *Kev Reynolds* Two books which cover the best of walking in the county. *ISBN 1 85284 156 7 200pp*

LONDON THEME WALKS *Frank Duerden* Ten fascinating walks based on popular themes. *ISBN 1 85284 145 1 144pp*

RURAL RIDES No.1 WEST SURREY *Ron Strutt ISBN 1 85284 272 5 192pp*

RURAL RIDES No.2 EAST SURREY *Ron Strutt ISBN 1 85284 273 3 160pp*
Bike rides for all the family, with a wealth of information and history

WALKING IN SUSSEX *Kev Reynolds* 40 walks in the great variety of scenery and history of Sussex. *ISBN 1 85284 292 X*

SOUTH WEST ENGLAND

WALKING IN CORNWALL *John Earle* Walks include the Coast Path, and the interesting interior. *ISBN 1 85284 217 2 200pp*

WALKING ON DARTMOOR *John Earle* The most comprehensive walking guide to the National Park. *ISBN 0 902363 84 0 224pp*

WALKING IN DEVON *David Woodthorpe* 16 coastal, 15 countryside and 14 Dartmoor walks. *ISBN 1 85284 223 7 200pp*

WALKING IN DORSET *James Roberts* Circular walks between 5 and 12 miles. Spectacular coastline, lovely downs and fine pubs. *ISBN 1 85284 180 X 232pp*

A WALKER'S GUIDE TO THE PUBS OF DARTMOOR *Chris Wilson & Michael Bennie* Walks from 60 Dartmoor inns. *ISBN 1 85284 115 X 152 pp*

EXMOOR & THE QUANTOCKS *John Earle* Walks for all the family on the moors, valleys and coastline. *ISBN 1 85284 083 8 200pp*

WALKING IN SOMERSET *James Roberts* Gentle rambles to strenuous hikes, on Exmoor, the Quantocks and the pastoral lowlands. *ISBN 1 85284 253 9 280pp*

These are just a selection of books from the Cicerone catalogue, which covers most of Britain, Europe and many worldwide destinations. Send for catalogue to: CICERONE PRESS, 2 Police Square, Milnthorpe, Cumbria, LA7 7PY. Tel: 015395 62069 Fax: 015395 63417 E-mail: info@cicerone.demon.co.uk Website: www.cicerone.co.uk

PRINTED BY CARNMOR PRINT & DESIGN, PRESTON, U.K